W9-BVN-153

New Steps to Service

Common-Sense Advice for the School Library Media Specialist

ANN M. WASMAN

AMERICAN LIBRARY ASSOCIATION
CHICAGO AND LONDON
1998

The paper used in this publication meets the minimum requirements of American National Standard for Information Sciences—Permanence of Paper for Printed Library Materials, ANSI Z39.49-1992. ∞

Project manager: Joan A. Grygel

Cover and text design by Lesiak Design

Composition by Douglas & Gayle Limited in ITC Garamond using QuarkXpress 3.32

Printed on 50-pound White Offset, a pH-neutral stock, and bound in 10-point coated cover stock by V. G. Reed & Sons

Library of Congress Cataloging-in-Publication Data
Wasman, Ann.
    New steps to service : common-sense advice for the school library media specialist / by Ann M. Wasman.
        p.   cm.
    Rev. ed. of: Steps to service / Mildred L. Nickel, Rev. ed. 1984.
    ISBN 0-8389-3483-8
    1. School libraries--United States--Handbooks, manuals, etc.
2. Instructional materials centers--United States--Handbooks, manuals, etc.   I. Nickel, Mildred L.   Steps to service.   II. Title.
    Z675.S3N63   1998
    025.1'978--dc21   98-16248

Copyright © 1998 by the American Library Association. All rights reserved except those which may be granted by Sections 107 and 108 of the Copyright Revision Act of 1976.

Printed in the United States of America.

02 01 00 99 98   5 4 3 2 1

Sometimes we are blessed with some in our lives who keep us going when we're not sure we want to. To them, I dedicate this book.

Ben Wasman, my ever-suffering mate who is always—patiently, lovingly—there for me

Lois Kelly, my mom, whose energy, curiosity, and tenacity will, I hope, become more part of me as the years go by

Samantha, a yellow Labrador, and Paddy O'Rourke, a Bearded Collie, who constantly make me laugh and lavish me with unquestioning love

Buoyed by love, supported by family and friends, we can *all* be whatever we want.

Contents

Figures

Preface

This book, like its predecessors, is intended primarily for those new to the library media field. The first *Steps to Service* in 1975 and its revision in 1984 were noted for their practicality. This revitalization will continue with easy-to-read, easy-to-implement, sensible advice for handling basic day-to-day library media operations.

My own 30-plus years of experience as a school librarian as well as visits with library media specialists, new and experienced, at their library media centers (LMCs) and at conferences have formed a basis for many of the revisions in this work. While things have certainly changed since I stepped into my first library media position over three decades ago, the sense of frustration and the concern to perform well certainly have not. Today's new library media specialists face many of the same emotions and problems others have experienced over the years. However, they also immediately encounter a wealth of resources, technology, and equipment that many of the rest of us have had an opportunity to absorb gradually as part of our jobs.

Perhaps the first thing a newcomer must recognize is that a library media center is as individual as the school within which it operates. Its uniqueness is created by the staff, students, and curriculum it supports. Its functions may be complex in one area and relatively simple in others. Staffing patterns, budgets, materials, and size vary dramatically, but the "personality" the center inevitably takes on is set by the library media specialist.

While no preset "cookie cutter" system applies to every library media center, routine procedures are used in all. Obtaining, organizing, disseminating, and managing the items, functions, purposes, and activities of the library media center are based on a common framework. Although the details embellishing that frame must necessarily change from situation to situation, the concepts are the same. Whether cataloging is vendor-produced, computer-generated, or manually created on site, it is based on the same rules. Whether books are circulated by a manual or an electronic system or by clerical staff, the specialist, or an honor system, the purpose and process are similar.

Library users can move from library to library with little interruption. They can function, find and use materials, and obtain necessary information regardless of the library. This transfer is possible because of the standardized system within libraries, even though the libraries themselves may be dramatically different.

The same concept applies to setting up and operating library media centers. Regardless of their differences, the operating concepts are the same. Therefore, the procedures established in one center will apply to the next, so that what is learned and used in one job is applicable elsewhere. What a newcomer does on the first job can become precedent-setting for future positions. But getting off to a good start is not always easy. Hopefully, this book will help.

This work does not contain all answers to all questions. Its potential usefulness is based upon several assumptions. The reader

- is either relatively new to the field of library media or seeks a practical review of basic tasks
- recognizes that this book is a first step toward developing a quality library media program that fulfills its educational objectives
- is committed to doing a good job in his or her position and is willing to use other resources to activate that commitment

As technology continues to change and expand our world, the steps presented in this book will change and, in some cases, become extinct. Some already are dying; for example, the majority of LMCs today do not maintain traditional card catalogs. However, for the newcomer in a small facility with no hope of obtaining an automated system in the near future, knowing how to keep a traditional card catalog current and useful is vital. Thus, this seemingly outmoded step is included.

Chapter 1 begins with a brief look at the development of library media centers. Understanding how the history and purpose of library media programs have evolved can be helpful, especially if you accept a position in a facility that has not yet emerged from the early stages of development. Being aware of the library media field's background can also give you a sense of belonging and becoming.

Another bit of necessary background is a knowledge of the standards and guidelines developed by the American Association of School Librarians (AASL) and the Association for Educational Communication and Technology (AECT), described in chapter 2. These guidelines are explained so that their position in the field's development—past, present, and future—is understood by those who will actively be part of that continuing development. Determining where we will be rests in large part on where we have been.

Chapter 3 looks at the resources available to set oneself philosophically into the mold and mind of a library media specialist. More practical details emerge in chapter 4: how to prepare for a position, what to do before the school year gets under way, and how to survive the first week.

The major portion of this book, parts II and III, deals with the everyday routines that must inevitably be performed so that a library media center can be useful on a regular basis. Such routines are presented with a predisposition to those in facilities that are smaller—in collection, budget, and size—since these schools are less likely to offer any type of on-the-job support. It is also important that you recognize that each chapter in this work is an overview, an introduction. You must seek in-depth coverage of the topic from other sources by using the recommendations in the appendixes.

Since each library media center is different, the type of information sources, equipment, and technology is also different. What a specialist needs to know in one situation may be drastically different from what that same individual would need to know in another situation. This book cannot resolve all those differences but concentrates on the fact that the process is the same. For example, some school library media centers are the focal point for Internet access in their buildings, setting up numbers of computer stations for student Internet use, while other LMCs rely on more-traditional print sources. Whatever the source, the evaluation, interpretation, and synthesizing of information is the same, and that process is where library media specialists must concentrate their energies. The information source will change; the process will not.

The book is divided into sections including Handling Materials, Dealing with Details (administrative), and Working with People—staff, students, administrators, and parents. There is inevitable overlap. An idea mentioned in one section that has implications for another is not necessarily repeated. The index will help you identify these jumps.

While there is an attempt to present information logically, the way a novice might approach the tasks, this book is not designed to be a sequential experience. You are encouraged to skip those chapters that describe procedures about which you are knowledgeable. This work is a handbook, a guide, a helpmate that will be there if and when it is needed.

Acknowledgments

This book was inspired and assisted by special individuals, and I thank them.

Donald Adcock, whose talent, commitment, and professionalism should be a guide for all members of the profession

Linda Hartman, whose assistance, enthusiasm, and pure joy in her profession, her family, and her life make her a valued colleague

Carolyn Gudgeon, the sister I never had, who quickly surpassed me in library media with her grasp of our sometimes tenuous positions within education

James Harvey, whose wit and advice have ever corrected my path

All have lent their opinions, their time, and their encouragement.

Part *I*

Getting Started

1

Where did we come from?

Progressing from then to now

It often seems that to fully appreciate where we are, and to give direction to where we're going, we need to remember from whence we came. This advice seems especially pertinent to those embarking on a career in school library media work because our field recently has changed rapidly. What follows is the author's version of the development and purpose of school library media programs in the United States, tempered by the fact that only thirty years of it is based on personal experience.

In the beginning libraries were for the rich; only they had the time and money to spend reading and pursuing education. As the populace grew, its desire to have what the rich had—an education—also grew. By the late 1800s librarians had finally found their voices and had begun to advocate library service. Public libraries grew and, eventually, so did school libraries.

In elementary schools the beginnings were, logically, classroom collections, since schools began as one room with one teacher. As schools expanded, teachers continued to provide books for the students in their classrooms. As growth persisted, some schools decided to provide minimal funding for these collections, but teachers kept on (some even to this day) adding titles that were exclusively for "their kids." Finally, when schools reached a size that permitted them to diversify positions and hire administrators, it was recognized that a more economical and efficient method was to put all the books in one room so that all students could use them. However, many teachers clung to their classroom collections.

At the secondary level many libraries, especially in smaller, less-prosperous schools, began in the back of the study room. Whoever had study hall duty was responsible for circulating the books. Often an English teacher was given the task of organizing and ordering the materials. However, as collections and student populations grew, and as high schools became a stepping stone to additional education rather than the end of the educational cycle, separate rooms were established for the books.

Obviously, a separate room brought about the need for a caretaker to be responsible for the books. That individual may have been a school secretary, a dedicated teacher willing to put in extra time, or a parent; usually it was a quiet female content to take a back-room role. Eventually, in more progressive schools or those with larger collections, the position became a full-time job.

Training specifically intended for school librarianship was lacking and, to many, unnecessary. The school library's purpose was warehousing; the duty of the person in charge was organizing, circulating, and controlling. Few saw the need for any specialized training. This situation continued, in most cases, until the mid-twentieth century. Libraries were needed in schools, but recognition of their place within education and of the need for a trained individual to be in charge was ignored.

The educational changes brought about by World War II inevitably affected school libraries. The development of new teaching methods, accompanied by varied print and expanding nonprint materials, had an impact on how schools taught and on the quantity of items available to support that teaching.

As the 1950s began, the country was experiencing a stronger, more widespread prosperity than ever in history. The desire for education, the thirst for information, and the large numbers of students, coupled with the availability of increasing quantities of print and nonprint media, pushed education and libraries farther than they had been moved for some time.

AUDIOVISUAL EMERGES

For school libraries a new problem was emerging. As audiovisual (AV) materials and equipment began to flood the schools, another storage/keeper role emerged: the audiovisual specialist. The logical step would have been to place all audiovisual materials and their paraphernalia within the library under the care of the librarian. However, the equipment required the services of someone comfortable with operating and repairing it, and the female who worked so well with the books just didn't seem ready to work with the equipment's weight and complications. Therefore, a separate position, usually assigned to a male, was established at the secondary level. As in the case of libraries, the AV individual was often an overworked teacher who added this responsibility to his existing duties and was given a closet or small room for storage and repair. In the elementary school the classroom teachers or the principal assumed this responsibility.

During this period the warehouse function of the library did not change. However, the role of the librarian expanded somewhat, and training for school librarians become more important. No longer was the school librarian simply to keep the warehouse in order; now she was also expected to encourage reading. She was not seen as a teacher of reading but as a consultant to help students find appropriate books. However, her teaching function was activated as she showed students how to use the library for research.

The high school audiovisual specialist was also a warehouse keeper and a machine repairman, but his duties included teaching teachers how to use the new AV equipment and materials. At the elementary level, teachers learned from the principal or each other, since librarians were sparse and audiovisual specialists even rarer. At the college level, AV courses, devoted primarily to operating equipment, were added to teacher training programs.

In the late 1950s filmstrips, phonograph records, and 16mm movies reigned, but during the 1960s a new explosion occurred. Technology was on the move, changing the equipment and materials—in types of formats, availability for educational purposes, and quality of product. Books were also undergoing a revolution. Quantity and quality were increasing, and the paperback was making a dramatic inroad, offering an inexpensive source for titles of limited life.

At the same time, the United States developed an education conscience. The war parents of the 1940s, highly supportive of education, pushed their children toward college-prep programs. When Sputnik was launched in 1957, the USA's competitive spirit strongly reacted. We *had* to be better, to be first, to let the world know we were able to keep up with, and surpass, the Soviets. We had to improve our education and, with it, our school libraries.

FUNDING IMPROVES

The Elementary and Secondary Education Act passed in 1965, and for the first time large quantities of money flowed into public schools and their libraries. The educational community was bombarded with new educational devices, and educators struggled to bring all these potential wonders to the schools. Teachers felt increasing pressure to produce quality students and sought the best methods and materials to accomplish this goal.

Librarians stocked their shelves with up-to-date materials for reading and research, having demonstrated that their collections of aged books were not helpful to modern students. Audiovisual specialists, previously strapped by the considerable expense of equipment, used the influx of funds to purchase machines and materials in quantities that could be used by more teachers to reach more students than ever before. The "library ladies" and the "AV guys" fought for the same funds, each trying to prove his or her needs were more beneficial to the school. The solution was an uneasy alliance, each seeking to build his or her own area, yet both recognizing that materials, regardless of format, were important to teach students.

During the 1970s federal funds began to wane. Local districts picked up some of the slack, but budget constraints prevailed. Librarians realized that the best route was to merge their functions with the audiovisual specialists, who were not necessarily cooperative. Led by their professional associations, librarians advocated that *one* facility with a merged collection of *all* materials be established with *both* professionals operating within its parameters.

New terms were coined: *media, media center, media specialist.* New certification was created for a merged position with background in both areas. Unfortunately, not all librarians and audiovisual specialists accepted this concept, and isolated high schools retained a separate AV department. At the elementary level some librarians, where they existed, absorbed the new terminology and new tasks, while in other schools the teachers continued to be responsible for the nonprint format.

Simultaneously, some teachers and librarians, who reluctantly accepted the merged functions and facilities, resented the new terminology. They liked the tradition and reliability of the term *library.* A few went so far as to forbid student use of audiovisual materials as research sources. The relationship between AV and library, for these few, was very strained.

Merging the functions was not as easy as merging the facilities. The librarian recognized the value of cataloging and circulating audiovisual material, but the formats did not fit the usual cataloging/processing techniques or the standard shelving. The audiovisual specialist was uncomfortable with the print materials and reluctant to undertake the traditional librarian role, but the reverse was not usually true. The merger eventually led to the decline and fall of the audiovisual department as a separate entity.

The new media center became a more active facility as teachers grew more aware of, and reliant on, audiovisual materials for individualized instruction. Warehousing was no longer the only function of the center; more and more it was becoming a place of learning. The role of the media specialist was also changing. In addition to the warehouse function, the reading guidance role, and teaching library skills, the specialist now had to know the strengths and weaknesses of all materials and use that knowledge to teach staff and students. Teachers and media specialists were beginning to work as teammates.

With isolated exceptions, the merger of AV and library became the norm of the 1980s. Budget problems not only continued for library media programs but expanded to encompass the entire school. Irate taxpayers demanded more for their money,

convinced that schools were unaccountable and overly expensive. They insisted on a return to the "basics" of education, claim-
ing students no longer understood fundamental knowledge. Media programs reacted by developing more cost-conscious
systems as the prices of materials and equipment soared.

TERMINOLOGY CLASHES

Those holdouts in the profession who had retained the term *library* pointed out that the public, wondering what had happened to the library, was suspicious of the new media terminology. These traditionalists also noted that media, to the public,
usually referred to the mass communication agencies, who were
not always a respected entity. Thus, a compromise was born in
the terminology *library media,* allowing the views of both traditionalists and those concerned with the new technology to be accommodated.

Computers, which had begun to penetrate public education
in the 1970s, continued to expand into the school marketplace,
setting off an educational revolution that outweighed the one after World War II. With reluctance by many, teachers used the
new technology, finding that their students took to it with un-
abashed curiosity and unbelievable understanding. Adventurous
library media specialists evaluated the new technology, seeing in
it a potential to free themselves from clerical tasks and to use
their time more effectively within the educational process.

However, the possibilities offered by computers didn't stop
with clerical functions; it soon became evident they represented
another type of resource useful for student education, much as
AV materials had a couple of decades earlier. As had happened
with the audiovisual field, a new position emerged in some
schools: computer technologist. In other schools the library media specialists became the catalysts and coordinators for computers. Therefore, in the 1980s some retained the previous roles
of warehouse keeper, reading consultant, and library-skills
teacher as well as materials specialist. They also added a new di-
mension, often becoming leaders in using and incorporating the
new computer technology into education. In a few other schools,

as had happened with audiovisual specialists, the computer technologists operated separately from the library media center.

In the 1990s school reform emerged as a number-one priority, pushed by a public increasingly critical of educational efforts. "Active learning," "student-centered learning," and "student products" became the buzz words. The advance of technology accommodated the changes of teaching method as students used computers to enter the Internet and the World Wide Web, finding resources in depth and numbers beyond anyone's dream. Budget-conscious community members, aware of the easy access to overwhelming information sources, began to question why the library media center and its personnel were necessary.

A DICHOTOMY

Library media specialists quickly recognized that the strength of computer technology was also its weakness: overwhelming volume with little or no organization. Library media specialists' strength in dealing with information gave them an advantage the classroom teacher and the computer technologist did not have, thus increasing the value of library media specialists as teammates. Together teachers, computer technologists, and library media specialists could teach students how to access and utilize information effectively and how to develop the thinking skills required to be rational, responsible members of society. And so a new purpose emerged for the library media program . . . and a new role for its staff.

Today there are still classroom collections in many elementary schools. Some of these are created with the assistance of a library media specialist who maintains a central record, catalogs the materials, and makes them available to all students in the school. Unfortunately, though, there are still isolated collections that are available only to the students in that room, hidden from the library media specialist, if there is such a person, and jealously guarded by the teacher.

The sad fact is that elementary schools have not developed library media facilities, collections, and staff at the same pace as secondary schools. According to research, about 25 percent of all schools—the majority being elementary—have no professionally prepared school library media specialists.[1] The number grows if we add "full-time" status. However, all is not perfect at the secondary level either. Although standards from accreditation agencies have pushed secondary schools into better library media situations, budget constraints have taken a toll in reducing collections and, worse yet, staff.

Regardless of the staffing pattern, regardless of the situation the newcomer must enter, children still need to learn and still need the expertise and assistance of a library media specialist. The evolution of the profession over the years is a credit to those who have cleared the way and who have dedicated their professional lives to creating a service that is indispensable to quality education. The library media program in any school is a direct reflection of the talent, commitment, and philosophy of the person in charge, whose tasks are many and ever-changing.

---

1. National Center for Education Statistics, *Survey Report: School Library Media Centers in the United States: 1990–91,* Washington, D.C.: U.S. Dept. of Education, Office of Educational Research and Improvement, Nov. 1994.

2

Where are we going?

Standards as a road map

How do school library media specialists know if their programs are effective? While teacher and student response is certainly one indicator, objective criteria are probably more helpful. Standards or guidelines developed by associations at the state, regional, and national levels have filled this role. They serve a viable purpose in the library media profession as markers on the road to improvement.

To the library media specialist, standards represent the authority and philosophy of the association, a body to be respected. To the profession, standards capsulize where the field should be. To the administrator, standards present a potential action plan in terms they can understand. To the community, standards are a guarantee that someone in education is focused on quality.

Standards are meant to be used, to bring to a library media program a measure of where the program is and where it should go. Standards that sit on the shelf so a library media specialist appears to be current in professional thinking are an insult to those who spent the hours and energy creating them. Standards that are read, then immediately ruled out as impossible to achieve, are a cop-out on the part of the reader.

Standards are designed to be an action plan for any library media situation. The library media specialist assumes two roles: that of initiator to develop the plan and that of catalyst for its implementation. It is his or her responsibility to decide which standards to use based on which has the most credibility for the school staff and the most usability for the situation. The library media specialist must become completely familiar with the selected standards, share them with the proper individuals, and designate whatever process will be used to develop and implement them.

Throughout the years that standards have been used, there have been noticeable trends in their development. Chief among these is that standards have demonstrated where the profession is and vice versa, reflecting changes and technological advances. Standards have pushed the profession forward, identifying problems and presenting solutions for those astute enough to interpret them. Those library media specialists who have used the standards effectively have improved their programs and their image. Those who have ignored the standards, in all likelihood, are stuck in the warehouse function.

AT THE STATE LEVEL

A logical first source for objective, unbiased standards or guidelines is the state agency that is responsible for education. The state agency establishes policies, procedures, rules, and criteria to implement educational laws as passed by the state legislature. Unfortunately, the majority of states do not mandate library media programs, so their criteria for facilities, collections, and staff are only recommendations. These recommendations are often minimal at best and should be used as a benchmark for a program in the beginning stages of development. As a beginning, however, you should contact the state department of education, request any existing standards for library media programs, and guarantee that the program meets them.

Another source of standards is the state school library media association. State associations frequently develop criteria patterned after national guidelines but adapted to their state's situation. Again, these are criteria you should obtain and review, although they, like most standards, do not bear the weight of mandates.

AT THE REGIONAL LEVEL

Regional accrediting agencies have developed criteria for school library media programs as part of their evaluation of a school for membership. While these agencies began primarily as accrediting agents for senior high schools, they have also developed criteria for elementary, junior high, and vocational schools. Although their standards are also frequently at the lower end of development for a quality program, the forms and procedures they use for evaluation are often quite helpful.

The instrument used by regional accrediting agencies for self-evaluation of the local school contains a section for library media. Emphasis is on quality rather than quantity and on the school library media center as an activating source for the curriculum. The document usually includes the philosophy and objectives of the school, a community profile, and the way the library media program fits within that framework. The instrument also involves others in addition to the library media staff as part of the evaluative process. Adapting the self-evaluation document can be a valid way to rate a program, especially if it is used in conjunction with national standards from the American Association of School Librarians (AASL). To find out what instruments and resources are available in your area, contact the appropriate accrediting agency. (See appendix A for a list of these agencies.)

Regional or local standards developed by school library media specialists in a particular geographical area may also be available. Such standards may be created within a school district, a county, or a library system. Although designed for a specific area, they can also be useful to others. Because such guidelines give an indication of what these particular groups deem important and worthwhile, they may be helpful for program comparison.

AT THE NATIONAL LEVEL

The standards most professionals embrace are those created by national associations. These criteria reflect the philosophy and efforts of professionals from across the entire country. They are more comprehensive, progressive, and visionary in their content than those at the state, regional, or local level may be.

In the 1920s a joint committee of the National Education Association (NEA) and the American Library Association (ALA) published standards for elementary and for high school libraries. The standards were revised into a single document in 1945. Both were essentially quantitative standards, indicating recommended size of the collection, staff, budget, facility, etc. Since their publication coincided with the phase when the library media center was essentially a warehouse and the collection was of primary concern, these quantitative measures were most appropriate at the time. They allowed the person responsible for the facility, as well as the administration, to measure specifically where the facility placed in terms of what seemed to be a proper collection.

The standards were revised in 1960, but they retained quantitative measures and dealt with collections, facilities, staff, and the program. In 1966 the Department of Audiovisual Instruction, now known as the Association for Educational Communication and Technology (AECT), issued quantitative standards for audiovisual programs only. In 1969 standards were published for the first time by the two associations, combining library and audiovisual into the media program, reflecting the thinking and action of that decade, and emphasizing people, programs, and access. These joint standards were revised in 1975, retaining the media terminology that reflected the program development at that point, and adding recommendations for district as well as school programs, stressing the interrelationships between the two.

When it was time for the next revision, something of monumental consequence happened: the format of the standards dramatically changed. *Information Power: Guidelines for School Library Media Programs,* published in 1988 by AASL and AECT, did not concentrate on quantities. Quantifying criteria were placed in the appendix, and the major portion of the document dealt with the role of the people responsible for the library media program. Although earlier editions had mentioned the functions and services of the school library media center, none had concentrated so intensely on what tasks the individual in the program should perform and what roles that individual should undertake.

The size of the budget, collection, and facility were not deemed unimportant but were seen in direct proportion to the activities of the individual in charge, to the role that person created for the program, to where the program fit in the total educational picture. *Information Power* stated that the library media specialist needed to perform three roles: teacher, information specialist, and instructional consultant. The document noted specific functions for each role. The information specialist function included

- providing access to the LMC
- providing adequate resources
- providing assistance in information location
- guiding users in selection of resources
- developing policies for resource use
- providing retrieval systems

The teacher function included instructing students, educators, and parents; the instructional consultant role included curriculum development, instructional development, and the use of technology. These three roles became the underlying foundation for all the activities the library media specialist undertook, but the information specialist role still received the most attention.

Information Power Revised

The 1998 version of national standards is another major breakthrough in standards development, resulting in two publications. The first one is *Information Literacy Standards for Student Learning,* an indication of what students must be able to achieve to be informationally literate. (An overview of these standards appears in appendix B.) The second publication is *Information Power: Building Partnerships for Learning,* which includes the student information literacy standards as well as guidelines on how to implement them through a quality library media program. For the first time, standards for library media programs are focused on, and revolve around, the learner.

Previous standards and guidelines have reflected a philosophy wherein the library media center is a necessary support for educational structure. But the 1998 guidelines, in reflecting what actually should be happening in the field, advocate the library media program as a vital part of the education program, a component of teaching and learning as important as any other area.

The 1998 guidelines also emphasize the role of the library media specialist. In this version the specialist has four functions:

1. information specialist who acquires and evaluates varied formats of resources and demonstrates locating, accessing, and evaluating information

2. teacher who works with students and others to analyze learning and information needs, finding and using resources for those needs

3. instructional partner who works as a teammate with fellow teachers to help students develop abilities in information use and communication

4. program administrator who manages all aspects of the collection and guides all activities of the program

Information literacy has finally been recognized as an essential part of learning. No longer do students parrot information they've found in varied sources as a test of how well they paraphrase and report. Now they use the information to become part of their own learning, today and tomorrow. They learn how to find information, evaluate it, use it, and then evaluate the total process to see if their results were worth their efforts. The vital force assisting them with that information-seeking process is the library media specialist.

The new standards and guidelines, when compared with the previous versions, reflect how the library media program has evolved. Initially a support for research, now the program is the center of all learning. The process of using information effectively is applicable to any subject at any time in any setting. Teaching this process is a team effort between the library media specialist and all other members of the education community.

It is essential that all library media specialists obtain these standards and guidelines, read them, adapt them, and make *Information Power: Building Partnerships for Learning* the primary authority for the library media program and their activities within that program. To obtain a copy contact the American Library Association, 50 E. Huron St., Chicago, IL 60611, or call (800) 545-2433.

3

How do I get "on task"?

Thinking and acting like a library media specialist

Whether you get a position through an application and interview or through an assignment change, realizing you'll be in charge of the library media center is a joyous moment. Being responsible for a school library media center is an exciting and demanding job, so this moment is a triumph to be savored. However, when the euphoria passes and the excitement begins to wane, reality sets in.

Being a library media specialist requires a tremendous amount of energy and expertise. Taking care of the needs of the entire staff and student body is not a small or an easy job. Being responsible for developing and improving a program, or just maintaining an existing one, can be a formidable task. Therefore, the best action at this point is to get busy *now*. Waiting until the first day of work is going to mean playing catch-up all year, an experience sure to leave a newcomer exhausted. There are plenty of other things to occupy the first few days besides trying to come up with an action plan to approach the job.

Some individuals have a philosophical problem about working before the official first day of the job. They are reluctant to give hours beyond those for which they are paid, but in library media positions extra hours just go with the territory. While teachers may take home piles of papers to grade and lesson plans to prepare, the library media specialist puts in extra hours at the workplace because it is impossible to take the library media center home.

Being prepared, however, will relieve some of the pressure inevitably felt during that first week of work. Several sources, explained in the following sections, can facilitate such preparation. It is important to keep in mind, however, that while all these resources should be appraised, they cannot possibly be completely investigated before that first day. Instead, they should become part of an ongoing learning process that continues throughout your career as a library media specialist.

DISTRICT COORDINATOR

Some districts have the foresight to include a district library media coordinator in addition to library professionals at the building level. In such districts, this individual is involved in all aspects of administering the library media program, including hiring and training new personnel. If such an individual is within your district, call and make an appointment at once. Indicate that you want to quickly get in step with the philosophy, practices, and policies of the district as they apply to the library media center.

District library media coordinators are an invaluable resource in training a newcomer. Not only can they provide insight about the program's goals and major activities, they can recommend titles to read, places to visit, activities to undertake first, and key people to meet and work with. They often have prepared materials about the processes recommended for use within the district. They are a source for advice or, if need be, a shoulder to cry on when, inevitably, something doesn't go as planned.

VISITING YOUR NEW LMC

Obviously, the best place to learn about a new situation is in the facility itself. If the position has been secured before the end of the school year, it may well be possible to arrange a visit with the present library media specialist—if that person is leaving under happy circumstances. If, however, the individual has been asked to leave the position, it is best to avoid complications by asking the administrator about a potential visit.

A visit presents an opportunity to see the facility in action, to get a sense of how it is used, and to see the flow of traffic and the use of space. It is a chance to browse the shelves, see the collection, understand how it is arranged and shelved, and see how it works when in use. Use the card catalog or electronic catalog just as a patron would use it to assess its organization and its reliability. Peruse all aspects of the facility to get a sense of what is happening so that work can continue relatively uninterrupted when you take charge. Figure 3.1 is a checklist for such a visit.

Another advantage of a pre-job visit is being able to talk to the current library media specialist. Find out that individual's philosophy, approach to teachers, use of materials, and role within the educational program. You may want to use the person's approach as a model to emulate or, depending on the information, one to avoid. The visit offers time to establish a link with the individual as the first person in a network of contacts to develop. It is also possible the current person will introduce you to other staff members, point out those who will likely be allies and "prime" users, and share the little secrets and tricks that make the job easier. If the meeting goes well, find out what end of the year activities the individual will perform and what will be left for the fall. If time permits, volunteer to return at the end of the year and help out for a day.

Meeting the current library media specialist in person may not be possible. Besides being awkward if the person is leaving under less than ideal circumstances, the facility may just be too busy to accommodate time to talk. However, you should still be able to stop in just to observe. Also, you can always offer to come by before or after school hours.

If a personal visit is out of the question, make a phone visit or use e-mail. Set a time in advance, just like a personal visit, so that the library media specialist knows what to expect.

VISITING OTHER LIBRARY MEDIA CENTERS

Another alternative to visiting the future job site, especially if distance is a problem, is to visit other library media centers that are

Figure 3.1 Visit Checklist

Location

Ask for or create a map of the LMC. Identify the following:

- [ ] All collection areas: fiction, nonfiction, biography, paperbacks, AV, reference, periodicals, vertical file, all special collection areas
- [ ] Circulation desk, AV equipment storage, workroom, security system, catalog, classroom areas, offices, conference areas
- [ ] Student areas: all tables, chairs, carrels
- [ ] Electronic resources: catalog, CD-ROMs, computers
- [ ] Display areas
- [ ] Other areas

Collection

Look over each collection area.

Take notes on quantity and quality for each area and anything that stands out or catches your eye.

Look at professional titles for library media: books and periodicals.

Look over the shelflist. Find what selection guides are used.

Procedures

How is each of the following handled? What supplies are used? What documentation exists?

- [ ] Circulation of each collection area
- [ ] Student usage by class, small group, individuals
- [ ] Scheduling of usage by teachers
- [ ] Circulation of AV equipment
- [ ] Overdues, lost, damaged materials
- [ ] Ordering and budget—equipment and materials
- [ ] Cataloging and processing—What classification materials are used?
- [ ] Instruction: frequency, role of the specialist, bibliography development
- [ ] Discipline
- [ ] Regular communication with staff, students, administration, parents— examples: newsletter, list of new materials, annual report
- [ ] Relation to district or other facilities (library system, etc.)

Impressions

- [ ] Appearance of student-accessible areas of the center
- [ ] Appearance of the work area, offices
- [ ] Condition of any files and supply areas
- [ ] Faculty—attitude, usage patterns (visit the lounge; meet staff members)
- [ ] Students—attitude, ease in finding and using resources

more conveniently located. The purpose of such a visit is to become familiar with how a library media center is set up and managed and to talk to an active library media specialist to obtain practical advice. The visit checklist can be used here also.

Visiting a couple of centers, preferably at the same grade level as the one to be assumed, is an excellent way to figure out what works and what doesn't. Taking notes, writing out personal reactions, interviewing specialists—all are preparation for the job to be undertaken. How many of these visits, for how long, or even if they are undertaken is up to you. Perhaps a new teacher does not go through this same type of preparation, but a new teacher is not responsible for the information needs of every student and staff member in the building.

NETWORKS

An especially valuable source of information for anyone in the field, regardless of whether or not they are experienced, is a network of other library media specialists. No one else will understand the problems, relish the accomplishments, or brainstorm the solutions better than someone who has been, or is, active in the same type of situation. Establishing the network as soon as possible will make the transition to the job much easier and will provide a psychological shoulder to cry on when the inevitable bad day or bad incident pops up.

Finding these kindred spirits is not as difficult as it may seem. It just takes a bit of boldness and effort. The first step is to find out if there is a local professional library group. If no one at the school of new employment knows, there are other schools in the area to contact as well as the local public library or library system. While school library media specialists would be the most logical source, librarians of all kinds will share many of the experiences that lie ahead.

Another good local source is retired library media staff members. The experience of these individuals is extremely helpful, and they often have the time to answer questions and give advice. They may even be encouraged to volunteer in the center for a while to assist you.

Help is also available through the Internet. LM_NET is an electronic discussion group that serves the school library community. Begun in June 1992, it is open to all individuals interested in the school library media field. Subscription is as easy as sending the command SUBSCRIBE LM_NET followed by your first and last names to LISTSERV@LISTSERV.SYR.EDU. After confirmation, access to a wealth of knowledge and advice from all over the globe is instantly available.

The next step, even if local and electronic support is available, is to join the state or national association. Becoming an active member who attends conferences and workshops and reads the publications is a wonderful way to put problems in perspective and to meet exceptional, involved people who will become an important part of professional existence. AASL is an especially focused group whose publications and activities can help the newcomer. A profile of this group can be found in appendix C.

While there is no guarantee that networking will provide answers to all questions, particularly at the moment the answer is needed, do not hesitate to set up your own network. Getting started on it will make you instantly feel a part of the field and will establish a career-long pattern of assistance and assurance.

READING

Whether or not visits and networks are possibilities for job preparation, you can always read. While some individuals may have been surrounded by textbooks as they took courses to prepare for a position, there is still more to read. Many of those texts can be reread; readers often discover their textbooks seem to have more meaning and make more sense when a job is looming on the horizon.

Primary among the titles to read is *Information Power: Building Partnerships for Learning,* the national standards. This document is an excellent way to discover exactly what a program should be, what it should do, how it relates to the total educational program, and what the role of the library media specialist should be. The standards include a bibliography of other potential sources that should be gleaned for additional reading materials, based on your own interests. Asking others in the field for suggested titles for prime reading is also a good strategy. When time permits, it may also be helpful to become more grounded in the purpose of education. The relationship between educational programs and the LMC can be better understood when viewed from the overall perspective. A good beginning is the national goals for education that can then lead to an understanding of the individual school's purpose. An astute library media specialist can then determine where and how the LMC fits in. For such an educational overview, look at the summary in appendix D.

Some of the best sources for library media information are magazines. The library media field has a number of helpful titles, and eventually you will figure out which ones are most important to you. Some are specific to grade level, some not; some cover specific areas such as computers, book selection, public relations, etc. For the type of overall, general-information periodicals that help ground someone in the field, consider the titles listed in appendix E.

The reading material mentioned thus far will help establish a mindset about the profession and an understanding of its philosophy. However, another type of reading is, perhaps, more immediately pertinent: reading about the school and district where the job will be. It should be no problem to obtain a copy of the district's and school's mission statement, goals, and objectives. If the school has participated in an accreditation evaluation, borrow that document. All of these materials may be obtained from the district library media coordinator or, if there is no such person, the school principal.

A school yearbook, if one is published, is a good way to get a feel for the school itself. Also obtain in advance faculty and student handbooks, which are usually updated over the summer and readied for the beginning of school. Having an idea of the school's purpose helps you understand what is expected and allows you to begin considering your role in accomplishing the school's mission.

The library media center may also have printed materials that provide insight about the program's purpose and image as presented to its patrons. Review statements of purpose, goals, and objectives as well as any handbooks or usage guidelines prepared for teachers or students. Browsing such material, taking notes on items of interest or concern, will help you avoid that "what do I do now?" feeling. A list of items that should be obtained for review is shown in figure 3.2.

EDUCATION

The last advice anyone who may have just finished coursework for job preparation wants to hear is to consider taking a course. However, for someone who hasn't had coursework recently (or at all), it's an excellent way to get into the swing of things. For all parties, whether just out of school or far, far away from such endeavors, a workshop on a pertinent topic can be a great beginning step.

The advantage of taking a library media course is that it gets you "psyched up," thinking about the work world and dealing with problems that now are not merely speculative. A course also can get you thinking about research and solving problems —both useful skills with which to begin a job. Being a member of a class makes you recognize what a student's world feels like, obviously a great asset when working with students. Classes are also a built-in network of people contacts—people who'll help solve problems and lend sympathy when things are not going well.

Workshops are excellent for individuals who have limited time, have specific needs, or simply want to meet others with similar interests. Workshops may be offered by universities, colleges, community colleges, businesses, or professional associations. The advantage of participation is that they are one or two days in length, focus on a very specific topic, and usually include breaks and meal functions that provide great opportunities to network with others. The topic does not have to pertain to library media; it can be an issue that has relevance to the job— such as time management, computer usage, stress relief, or handling personnel. Granted, in such cases the individuals involved may not be library media specialists, but a good network includes people with a variety of skills.

Figure 3.2   Items to Obtain or Create for Review

Philosophy and purpose
Anything pertaining to district, building, or program level, such as
- ☐ Mission statement
- ☐ Goals, objectives
- ☐ Plan for development
- ☐ Curriculum guide or outline by subject or grade
- ☐ Teaching model adopted by district, if any
- ☐ Standards used as guide for program development
- ☐ School board policies and procedures

Collection
- ☐ Inventory—last two
- ☐ Processing/cataloging procedures
- ☐ Equipment list
- ☐ Periodicals list
- ☐ List of symbols used for collection identification
- ☐ Selection policy and guidelines
- ☐ List of selection guides available
- ☐ Policy and forms for challenged materials

Circulation
- ☐ Procedures and forms for all types of materials
- ☐ Procedures and forms for overdues and lost or damaged items
- ☐ Procedures and forms for equipment usage
- ☐ Circulation statistics for past two years
- ☐ Manual for automated system (if there is one)
- ☐ Interlibrary loan procedures and sources

Budget
- ☐ Budget requests for three years—present, past, and future
- ☐ Budgeting manual and procedures for building and district
- ☐ List of funding sources other than regular budget
- ☐ Requisition form, purchase order form, and order cards or forms
- ☐ Accounting records for the LMC

Personnel
- ☐ List of any staff: paid, volunteer, and student
- ☐ Procedures and forms for procuring and evaluating staff members

Public relations
- ☐ Any written plan
- ☐ Annual report—past two years
- ☐ Copies of any newsletters, programs, projects, news articles, etc.

Preparing yourself by visiting, networking, reading, and taking courses is an excellent way to get ready for a job that will require more work, more energy, and more commitment than one could believe possible. It is also a job that will yield satisfaction and a greater sense of being part of something worthwhile and useful than one could anticipate.

ADDITIONAL PREPARATION

Being ready to do the job in a manner that assures students and staff you know what to do is impossible without spending time preparing for the job. Getting a library media mindset and finding practical and emotional support may make you feel ready, but they are not enough to get the job done. It is now time to review practical preparation for the tasks at hand.

Realistically, at the beginning of the job the key to providing service and obtaining staff support is to know the resources—what they are, where they are, how they circulate, and what, if any, changes need to be made. While it is generally not a good idea to make a lot of changes the first year, it is also wise not to continue a practice that seems totally foreign. For example, if there is a manual checkout system and your predecessor filed all cards for all materials alphabetically under the author's last name in one continuous file, regardless of due date or material type, such a system may be aggravating to say the least. Or perhaps the system has every card filed by date due with a separate area for *every* category of material—fiction, nonfiction, stories, AV, etc. Either example might impede operation and test your tolerance. Therefore, change to something usable, convenient, and sensible for how you will work.

Consider these scenarios: Your predecessor, who had been there a while, knew all the staff members and didn't bother to keep records of audiovisual equipment loans, relying on memory. Perhaps the library media specialist demanded that the equipment be returned at the end of each school day and checked out again the next morning, even with individuals who used the same equipment every day. Neither of these situations is totally workable, so a new system must be established.

What new system is used depends on what is workable for the person in charge, with possible suggestions from the sources mentioned previously: reading, networks, visits. Obviously this is yet another circumstance for which a district library media coordinator or another library media person in the district could give helpful advice.

Once the former specialist has departed, visit the LMC. Walk through the steps of those who use the LMC. If you notice a disruptive pattern, change it. For example, if the catalog is located at the opposite end of the facility from the circulation desk, maybe the catalog should be moved closer to the desk so someone is readily available to answer questions as searchers use it. If AV equipment is so far from the door that it must be rolled (inevitably with noise) past 90 percent of the seating area, maybe a new area can be created right next to a door. If a browsing area is set up by nonfiction although most browsers will use periodicals and short stories, you may need to move the furniture or the collection areas. Study all traffic patterns and locations for maximum use and convenience as well as security.

PAST RECORDS

A good beginning must include becoming acquainted with the collection, and one way to do that is to look over the most recent inventory. Begin with equipment, not because it is the most important of the many resources but because it is what many teachers will request at the beginning of the school year, some on the first day. To get off to an effective start with equipment, see chapter 11.

Next, get acquainted with the materials collection.

Was anything new ordered at the end of the year or over the summer?

Where is it?

Is it cataloged and ready to go?

If there are no records of what was ordered, ask the principal for copies of any purchase orders issued for the LMC since April 1. Then start looking for the material.

Do the purchase records indicate a particular teacher requested a purchase? If so, send notices to each requester indicating what came in and how to obtain it for use. Catalog and process the material within the first week or two of school so requesters can use it (unless you're sure it isn't needed until later in the year). If teachers need material before it's ready, let them take it. However, keep a good record of who has what, and ask them to return it as soon as they are through.

After taking care of materials ordered for the new school year, start browsing the collection in the LMC. Again using the last inventory, notice what materials are available in terms of format and number of titles. Try to find circulation statistics for the previous two years to get a sense of what was used. Browse the shelves; look over the condition of materials. Pull some from the shelves, and glance through to get a sense of their condition. Learn the locations of each type of material and collection area so that students and staff will be correctly directed from the first day and so it's easy to find items when they are needed. The reference collection is especially important, because it is the backbone for many questions and research projects. See what titles are included, become familiar with their content and organization, and watch for any gaps.

If there is time and you still have energy (especially if there is an extended contract for extra days), conduct a quick inventory. Begin with the reference collection, then look over the areas of highest circulation in the previous years. Take notes of apparent gaps. For example, if the newest edition of an encyclopedia is five years old, a newer one should be purchased; if there is no world almanac, make a note to obtain one; etc. See chapter 5 for details of inventory.

Check the titles on the periodicals list.

Where have they been kept?

What is the policy on circulation?

How are periodicals checked in upon arrival?

Are back issues kept? For how long? Where?

Is there a periodical index? Which one? Which indexed titles are present?

Lastly, peruse any areas of the collection not yet analyzed: audiovisual, fiction, computer software, special collections, vertical file, etc. Note the organization, arrangement, condition, specific titles, duplicates, and subject areas with a significant number of titles. Knowing the collection helps build your confidence so that you can direct students and staff to the appropriate areas as well as find materials to help plan units with teachers.

THE PAYOFF

Getting ready for the job will take time and energy, but the payoff will be worth the effort. Time spent now is time saved when teachers and students are demanding your assistance. The worst feelings newcomers to a job can have in their first days include not knowing what they're doing, feeling they don't belong where they are, and sensing everyone is annoyed with their efforts.

The first day of work for the new library media specialist should be well *before* the rest of the staff comes in. Nothing impresses teachers more than a library media center that is ready for business, with all equipment and materials ready to circulate and to be used. Unfortunately, many teachers have become—reluctantly and resentfully—accustomed to the library media center being closed the first week or two of school while the library media specialist prepares the facility and conducts library orientation. Thus, a functional facility will be a welcome surprise and a big plus for the "new kid on the block."

4

How do I get through the first week?

Activities and priorities

A library media center with everything ready to go from the first day is of no use unless everyone who wants to use it *knows* it is available, especially if this has not been the case in the past. Announcing the LMC is ready can be done in one or more ways, all of which should be combined with an introduction to yourself, the new library media specialist. On that first day, which is likely to be teachers only, each teacher's mailbox should contain a jazzy flyer, a friendly memo, or an informal invitation to stop by the LMC to have lemonade and cookies and get acquainted.

Undoubtedly, there will be a faculty meeting the first day and, chances are, the new staff members will be introduced. This is an excellent opportunity to make a brief statement indicating that the LMC is ready for business, quickly identifying the usefulness of the program to the staff and, perhaps, mentioning a new service or material or some other "teaser" to entice visitors to the center. Checking with the principal *at least* a week in advance of this moment and limiting it to three minutes can set a precedent for other faculty meetings.

Some staff members will be at the LMC door even without an invitation; most of them will be demanding AV equipment they are accustomed to having for the year. Imagine their surprise when they find you have already anticipated and resolved this situation. Consider the impact of this gesture!

THE WELCOMING

Teachers often spend time before the school year starts making their rooms student friendly. They create bulletin boards and displays that reflect content the class will study and that encourage the students to get involved. Teachers may post welcome signs on the door or list students' names in a conspicuous place—all to make the students feel at home. The LMC should also create this welcoming atmosphere, but it must consider two groups: students and teachers.

Since teachers will be present the first day, a visible welcoming is another task to handle before school is officially under way. How much time you spend and how extensively you decorate are individual decisions. However, the LMC's environment should reflect its usefulness and its easy availability as well as the fact that the LMC is under new management.

If there is space outside the LMC's doors, design a display to encourage individuals to come *into* the facility. Obviously the entrance should be clearly identified as the library media center. Then, nearby, whether using a theme of "check us out," "the place to be," "the info place," the "resource store," or whatever else is appealing, use attractive eye-catching visuals to introduce both the LMC and yourself to students and staff. Maybe there's a display case or a bulletin board. If not, perhaps you can borrow a portable bulletin board. One sure-fire method is to feature photos, perhaps of new staff members, or if the staff is not large, of all staff members. A Polaroid camera will facilitate such a display to attract teachers as well as students.

If it feels uncomfortable to feature teachers this soon, use a photo essay to introduce yourself with tie-ins to materials in the LMC. Use baby and child photos and photos of high school graduation, college graduation, high school and college activities, family, and hobbies. Make captions for the photos, and place appropriate materials nearby. For example, let's say you played high school football. Display a photo of yourself with a caption such as "Made the team but I wasn't a stand-out. Sure could have used Ditka's advice." Then put Mike Ditka's biography in the case—or use the local coach's name and display a video of one of the team's games from the previous season.

The first days before students arrive is a logical time to get ready for them; that's what the teachers will be doing. But remember, when teachers are in the building, *they* become the priority and you should assist them whenever they come by—or actively seek them out. Going room to room, momentarily stopping for introductions, ask if there are any special requests concerning the LMC. Invite teachers to stop in the center (reinforced by the mailbox invitation and the faculty meeting). At the very least, this starts teacher relationships off on a positive note. It is also a good time to ask each teacher about any plans to bring students in during the first month so that preparations can be made.

In some schools the first month is occupied with library orientation, that traditional start-of-school experience. Such concentrated orientation has not been proven to be effective enough to displace the regular activities of the library media program. In fact, research indicates that any library skills or orientation taught in isolation from a specific information need are not worth the time it takes to teach. Students remember skills when they have to apply them, when they *use* the skill. Instructing where things are and how to use them when there's no purpose invalidates the process. Library orientation should be part of the student's first informational-need visit, but only to the degree to which students will use the items presented.

SCHEDULING AND CLASS USE

This brings us to a fundamental point: *How* is the LMC used?

Is there a flexible schedule wherein students and staff come and go as they need information?

Do classes get "booked in" when the teacher has a project
that requires the materials of the center and the
expertise of its specialist?

Are classes set up on a permanent schedule, visiting on
regular weekly cycles?

Some schools, unfortunately, use class time in the LMC to
give the classroom teacher a planning period or lunch period.
During these times the LMC is often closed to other students because there is no specialist available to work with them.

A top priority that first week, preferably sooner, is meeting
with the principal to discuss what system is used. If it is the
"scheduled" concept, incredulously ask what happens to students who have information needs if their need is during someone else's time. Point out you wouldn't be able to work with a
class and help individuals or small groups at the same time. Ask
the principal's advice about how to handle such a situation.
However, if the "schedule" has been a time-honored tradition, as
it is in nearly 65 percent of elementary schools, and the principal uses it to give teachers release time, there is little that can be
done the first year except to point out potential problems with
the system, fuss about the unmet information needs, and begin
preparing a strategy to replace the system.

Set up the scheduled classes but try to allow free time every
day, even if it's only a half hour, when students can come to the
LMC from any class for any information need. One way to get
such time is to shorten the scheduled LMC visits by 5 or 10 minutes each. Then emphasize and advertise the special time thus
created, working with teachers to develop projects to use such
time. Build in not only a lunch break but also another block to
use for the many tasks that must be accomplished when not
working with students. Alternatively, try to schedule classes so
that there is a day or half day open for flexible use and for your
library media tasks.

If the schedule is the same every week, create a chart show-
ing who comes when. Laminate it, post it, make copies, and distribute it. If the schedule has some variations week to week, use
a lesson plan book to keep track, and post the schedule weekly
in a conspicuous place so everyone can see what's going on.

Such visibility helps avoid the "what does that person do all day?" issue some teachers raise. See figure 4.1 for a sample schedule that includes three sections each of morning and afternoon kindergarten and four sections each for grades 1 through 5.

Quite often teachers are busy the first week preparing their rooms, meeting their students, planning lessons, setting the classroom tone, and establishing their expectations. Therefore, other than AV equipment and materials—or possibly the LMC computers—the demand for service and assistance may be light during this time. Thus, it is perfect for planning or catching up on any tasks not yet finished. (You've already dealt with material and equipment organization and circulation and the process for LMC usage by classes, groups, and individual students.) If any aspect is not ready to go, take care of it at once.

NOTIFICATION OF PROCEDURES

All usage procedures—whether for circulation or access to the LMC and its resources—should be clear to users, especially if anything has been changed from the previous year. For example, reminder signs near the circulation desk should indicate "ID required" or "sign first name, last name and room number [or teacher's name]." Some students always need a refresher, and new students need to know what to do. A procedure that students are expected to know should be visible to avoid problems created by the "no-one-told-me" syndrome.

If there is a certain way to use the computer equipment, post simple directions, making them appropriate for the grade levels that will be using them. For example, for lower grades you may want to create some simple illustrations or take photos of students performing the task, which you could then incorporate into written directions. You may also want to ask students to ask you to help create the directions. If students are expected to refile vertical file material, display a poster with such directions near the area. If students are not to reshelve books, a book truck marked "place books here" should be conspicuous. If there are behavior expectations, they should be posted. A map indicating where materials, equipment, and services are located should be

Figure 4.1 Sample Scheduled Classes for Library Media Center

Time	Monday	Tuesday	Wednesday	Thursday	Friday
Before school			Open to all students		
9:00–9:30	K-Kelly	1-Poppen	2-Behrens	4-Edwards	4-Pessina
9:40–10:10	K-Pattison	1-Robinson	2-Montgomery	5-Martin	5-Banks
10:20–10:50	K-Cross	2-Hartman	3-Layton	4-Kulp	
11:00–11:30			Open to all classes and students		
11:30–12:30			Lunch		
12:30–1:00	K-Kelly	1-Gudgeon	3-Wheeler	5-Parker	Open to all students
1:10–1:40	K-Pattison	1-Hauge	3-Altman	4-Wood	LMC WORK
1:50–2:20	K-Cross	2-Adcock	3-Hogan	5-Amato	LMC WORK
2:30–3:00			Open to all classes and students		
After school			Open to all students		

displayed near the entrance. Never assume everyone remembers; assume everyone needs a concise, visible reminder. And remember, you never know when a first-time visitor may arrive.

This first week is also the perfect time to notify teachers if there has been *any* change—in procedure, in location of items, in anything. In fact, even if everything is the same, create an attractive flyer or booklet outlining usage expectations, services, circulation information, hours, and other pertinent information and give it to all staff members including secretaries and custodians. Of course, you should prominently feature your name and a statement of your willingness to be of assistance. Having such material available to parents upon request and advertising its availability also increase the LMC's visibility.

The best way to avoid sticky usage problems is to anticipate them in advance and notify everyone about what is expected. Having procedures written out and distributed shows the principal that notification has been made. Remember, whatever is given to teachers should first be presented to the principal for his or her information. All these same procedures, plus any library media practices, should be written out and placed in an LMC procedures handbook for library media staff use. Review, evaluate, and update the handbook regularly.

The first week is also the beginning of establishing cooperation and involvement with grade levels or departments. Try to attend each group's meeting to get acquainted (or invite them to the LMC) and to ask about their needs, requests, upcoming units, and expectations. It's a good time to distribute procedural flyers or booklets. The more that is known in advance, the better the need can be met.

ORIENTATION

If you are expected to provide the traditional library orientation mentioned earlier, and avoiding it would create problems with staff members, work out an orientation schedule and activate it as soon as possible. Ask teachers which classes wish to come, what they expect to be covered, and how the students will use the information. Keep all sessions brief, use handouts that are informative and concise, and try to work with each teacher to create a specific information need so that students will use the information being presented. Maybe all they'll do is check out a book for pleasure reading, but that's enough to demonstrate (quickly)

- how to use the catalog to locate books by topic
- how to look up a favorite author or title
- how to check out and return materials
- the policies for overdues and damaged or lost materials
- two to three new titles that would be great reading

If scheduled classes are the rule, you're responsible for the lessons when students are in the LMC. First, you need to know what students already know about using the LMC. One way is to create worksheets that test their knowledge yet are also fun to do. The questions pertain to skills they might know, such as

- Looking in the dictionary, what is the word listed above the entry *pretty?*
- Using the card catalog, find a paperback book by R. L. Stine and write down the title.
- Using the *Readers' Guide to Periodical Literature,* identify an article about Mars exploration and write the title and date of the magazine it is in.

Obviously, the questions you create and the materials to be used will pertain to the age level of the children you're testing. For example, for primary elementary grades, you may use the new *Readers' Guide for Young People.*

Once you find out what students know, you can create lessons. You can concentrate on different subjects; you can read excerpts from poems or books; you can look at the styles of different illustrators and authors. There are books of activities such as these available for all grade levels that you may seek out and use.

There's no time like the first week to start getting acquainted with the students, especially if there are no scheduled classes for orientation or regular library times. Stand outside the door before and after school and at other times students are moving about. Smile, say hello, and invite them to stop in and see what's new. It's also a great way to observe your future clients.

Let students see that you are eager to work with them, but look and act professional. Although casual dress may be permitted on "teacher" days, a newcomer should approach such times conservatively, avoiding jeans and shorts and opting for a casual but professional appearance. When the students arrive, dress up a bit. Students should recognize the library media specialist as a friendly, caring staff member, not a peer.

When in the hallways, be as active in watching and caring for students as the teachers should be. If shenanigans occur, curb them. Familiarize yourself with school behavior expectations and enforce them. Don't become a policeman or a fanatic, but don't allow a student to walk by talking on a cellular phone if such equipment is forbidden in school. Develop a manner of dealing with students that reflects that you know and respect the rules but you don't intend to make "examples" of every student you see. Such a technique may take time, but it'll come with practice. Above all, do not hide out in the LMC, convincing yourself you have too much to do to meet and greet students.

The primary goals of the first week are to

- get acquainted with staff and students
- set the tone of how the LMC is to be used and operated
- establish a warm and welcoming atmosphere
- make all users aware that you are an individual who is willing and capable of helping
- make equipment and materials ready for those who need them

Part *II*

Handling
Materials

5

Do I really have to look at all this stuff?
Inventory

Inventory is the process of matching what is in the collection with what is supposed to be there. Taking inventory is the *best* way to learn a collection because it involves the physical task of touching items, looking at them, and accounting for them. Knowing what is available, in what quality and quantity, and how it is being used is invaluable, especially to a newcomer. Before addressing how to conduct an inventory, let's first dispel a few myths.

THE MYTHS

MYTH #1: Inventory should be conducted at the end of the year.

Not so, which is why this myth is number 1, near the beginning of a new person's activities for the year. Traditionally, school librarians have spent the last-gasp days of the school year diligently inventorying their collection. Some library media specialists wait for the end of the year because it's become a ritual of closing and a way to get everything in order for the next year. Some argue they need everything back before they can account for it, so they have to wait until nothing is circulating. Some claim it's the best way to know what's missing, so they can undertake a search for lost items before school dismisses for the year. But, realistically, inventory can be done at *any* time of the school year. For new library media specialists, the sooner the inventory is taken, the sooner they know the collection's strengths and weaknesses.

MYTH #2: The library media center must be closed to conduct inventory.

In their pursuit to account for every piece, many school library media specialists typically close the facility to regular use. Because such closure often coincides with the end of the year, teachers, who don't understand the concentration required for the process, become upset that the library media specialist is, to their thinking, "done" for the year. Students, who often leave assignments until the last possible moment, get disturbed when blocked off from the information sources they need. Parents, hearing their children are cut off from what their taxpayer dollars have bought, become angry. The bad PR thus generated from such closure taints much of the good work done during the school year.

The complaints do not necessarily go away if the inventory is conducted at another time. Again, realistically, the LMC does *not* need to close—depending on its staffing patterns. If someone is available to assist teachers and students, the LMC can remain open while others conduct the inventory. Obviously, if the only inventory taker is also the library media specialist, the LMC will have to close. Frequently there are teacher institute or inservice days that can be used for this task. School holidays could be used for inventory if a "comp" time or payment can be worked out. For example, some library media specialists, if they cannot get financial compensation or swap time off, will exchange holiday work days for time to go to professional conferences or school visits. However, if there's a collective bargaining agreement, such time arrangements need to be checked out with the teacher organization to be sure there is no contract violation.

MYTH #3: Everything must be inventoried at the same time.

This myth is probably the worst one because it has an impact on all the others. It logically follows that if everything is inventoried at the same time, then nothing is available, all energy is concentrated on this task, and the LMC may as well close. However, it has never been proven that taking a "whole" inventory is better than a piecemeal one. Personal experience has shown that doing a portion here and a portion there is better because inventory takers are less overwhelmed, exhausted, and bored, thus eliminating a lot of errors due to fatigue. They're also better able to focus on the particular section under scrutiny and are more sensitive to its problems. In addition, doing bits and pieces gives everyone involved a sense of accomplishment as they tick off the sections completed—an important morale factor. Naturally, doing sections can more easily facilitate maintaining regular usage . . . and happier patrons.

MYTH #4: The entire collection must be in perfect order before beginning inventory.

Again, if a section is inventoried, only that section needs to be in order. In truth, such order is not even necessary with most automated systems because they can track items wherever they're placed and even alert the inventory taker if something is misshelved. However, the process goes smoother with the section in order and accomplishes a dual purpose by making items more accessible for patrons. If the inventory is a manual process, perfect order *is* essential.

MYTH #5: Nothing can be checked out while an inventory is under way.

The purpose of an inventory is to account for an item. It doesn't matter if the item is in repair, on the shelf, or in a patron's possession; so long as it can be "accounted for" somewhere, the goal of the inventory is accomplished. However, since one of

of an inventory is to determine the physical con-
item, its being checked out negates that function.
flag can be put on the circulation record so the item
can be inspected when it's returned. Granted, it *is* easier to complete an inventory of a section if circulation of that area is curtailed until the account is taken. Doing a section at a time allows
the remainder of the collection to be available to patrons.

MYTH #6: Every item must be inventoried every year.

Every section has to be inventoried often enough to keep track
of it, but a yearly accounting is not necessary for most items. The
exception may be those sections that support critical curriculum
units. For example, maybe the entire school gets involved in a
major project on the Renaissance or the environment or the
ocean. Those materials need to be on hand and in good shape
every year, so a yearly inventory is justified. The reference collection is also an area that needs to be up to date and in good
repair because of its constant use.

Other portions of the collection can be done every other
year but not less often than every three years. Otherwise, the collection seems to get away from you and there's too much change
to deal with. The more often the inventory is done, the better the
grasp on its content and condition. However, you must also factor in your time.

MYTH #7: The reports generated from an inventory necessitate doing it.

Many school library media specialists undertake inventory because they think they should to generate reports of numbers of
materials on hand by category. They share these data with their
principal, demonstrating how they effectively keep track of materials. Some of these figures are then used by the administration
to assist in completing requirements for accrediting agencies.
However, some specialists discover such high loss figures that
they are afraid to let the principal see the results, so going to all

that effort just for a report is a waste of time. There are far more valid reasons to undergo the rigors and frustrations of inventory, as explained in the following sections.

Dispelling the myths about inventory, then, leads to the realization that a portion of the collection can be inventoried while regular LMC activities go on by using student nonattendance days or outside assistance.

REASONS FOR INVENTORY

Inventory is a necessary process, in spite of the time and effort it entails. In fact, sometimes we have to remind ourselves why we need to do it. The reasons outlined in the following sections are the most pertinent.

Knowing the Collection

Looking at each collection item, whether briefly by noting only titles or at greater length by actually scanning items, makes an impression on the mind. For most of us a little bell goes off as we file away the information: A certain title is there, a particular subject is covered in an unexpected book, or a curricular area is represented by a significant number of titles. We also internally note the lack of materials on topics or the currency (or lack of it) in critical areas.

We recall these bits and pieces of what is and what isn't in the collection as we answer reference questions, prepare bibliographies, or search for appropriate reading choices. Eventually such internal notes become a natural process unique to library media professionals, who realize their expertise in *knowing* the collection is a key factor in its being used.

Another seemingly natural action while doing inventory, one that also lends itself to collection knowledge, is the somewhat irresistible urge to look over titles in more depth: to note copyright dates, organization, coverage, format, and indexes. Again, this information resides in the brain, triggered by a particular question or assignment. For those whose recall powers may not be as strong, conducting an inventory accompanied by a note pad allows us to make notes about the resources we find. For example, suppose we find *The World's Greatest Scientists* in the collective biography section. Curious, we glance at the table of contents and note two mathematicians are included. We assume, probably correctly, that the subject heading for the title is *Scientists* or *Science-Biography* with no access point for mathematicians nor any analytical entries for each person. We make a mental note that is retrieved later when a mathematics teacher announces a unit on outstanding mathematicians. In another example, as we account for a videotape entitled *Architecture Today,* we glance at the summary on the box and see there's an entire section on bridges, again with no analytical entries in the catalog. The mental note we make is triggered when we discover the science classes require a bridge-building project.

"But," a newcomer may say, "I don't know the curriculum well enough to know any of that." That's one reason inventory is periodically repeated: We remember materials that will work with units we've encountered on the job. Second, many of us, when faced with a new project or unit, will recall from inventory, "Didn't I see something about that when I inventoried the *X* area?" and then look for it.

This building of collection knowledge, triggered by physical contact with materials at a time when your antennas are up to receive new information, is one of the great strengths of library media specialists. Thus, every library media specialist should personally inventory every collection area every three to five years—just to keep in touch with what's there.

Analyzing Patterns of Usage

Although circulation statistics can indicate what collection areas are circulated the most, inventory can determine how intense the usage has actually been. When organizing a section prior to inventorying it, if one area is particularly disheveled, it may indicate a lot of student activity in that area. On the other hand, a certain section may have a lot of items that are physically damaged. Both circumstances must be analyzed to see if the problem is vandalism or heavy use. If, for example, a look at circulation records (or the circulation card) shows that the item has been checked out frequently within a year or two, duplicates of the title—or additional resources on the topic—should be added to the collection.

Missing pages, sagging bindings, or missing pieces of a set also may indicate a usage need. If it appears students are "ripping off" particular items or sections, the problem may be that there isn't enough material available on the topic, so students became frustrated and took what there was rather than waiting for it to become available. For example, two titles about animals have the section on wombats missing. A further look shows that only three titles contained any information at all. Perhaps specific titles on the topics would help; definitely more materials are needed. Perhaps the materials need to be placed on reserve for the unit and check-in procedures need to be tightened. At the minimum, the damaged titles need to be replaced.

Evidence of heavy usage also leads to another aspect of the library media specialist's job: discussion with the instructors involved. Initiate conversation about the adequacy of the sources if students complain they can't find information or if the information isn't complete enough. Is time a factor? Should there be lengthier check-out times or more time allotted for the unit? Seeing the patterns that inventory shows, and following up on them, are reasons for doing an inventory that obviously go beyond just counting numbers and justifying records.

Analyzing Patterns of Missing Materials

Missing items lead to the same type of analysis and the same possible conversations as usage patterns do. In addition, missing materials raise another question: Should the item be immediately replaced? Scrutinize circulation records and curriculum units to determine how important the material is. If the item hasn't circulated for three years, past inventories need to be checked to see how long it's been missing. If it is part of a major unit for a teacher or grade, it should be replaced in time for the unit's next due date. If it does not seem to be a popular title or part of an important unit, it can go on a wait-and-see status. However, missing items should not be carried over for several years. Some library media specialists wait for the item to reappear, which they sometimes do. If a title is worth placing in the collection, it is worth keeping in the collection and should be replaced.

Justifying the Catalog and Shelflist

Occasionally, previous inventories have been sloppy or incomplete. The materials may be identified, but the records are not adjusted. This failure negates the inventory process because patrons will continue to identify the title mentioned and will continue to look for it even though the library media specialist knows it is gone. Conversely, some items appear on the shelf that are not in the records. The catalog, shelflist, or inventory-control record must be consistently adjusted to show which items are actually available.

Preparing for Weeding

Weeding is a separate function from inventory and may not necessarily be part of inventory. For example, when a newcomer is conducting a quick inventory to learn the collection it is not an appropriate time to become involved in weeding decisions. In a normal inventory process, materials are identified that may be candidates for weeding. Such items are usually obvious because of their physical condition, but sometimes their titles will compel you to look at them more closely. On the other hand, you may become curious about the large number of titles on a particular topic. Whatever the reason, the physical activity of dealing with the materials will result in marking some for weeding consideration.

CONDUCTING THE INVENTORY

Regardless of when the inventory is conducted, what portion is being accounted for, or who is to do it, there are certain preparations that need to be made. First of all, inventory takers should dress for a dirty job. Handling items that have been sitting on the shelves is not conducive to wearing good clothes. Before starting, read and straighten the shelves of the portion to be done; while this is not necessary, it is helpful. If this is a quick inventory conducted with an automated system, such preparation is not needed.

Next gather the following:

the shelflist for the section being inventoried—or a handheld scanner unit for the automation system (If you have no handheld scanner, you will need a book truck to load the materials and take them to the terminal to be scanned, unless your terminal can easily be disconnected and transported to the shelves.)

one or two extra book trucks to hold materials that may need additional consideration, repair, or cataloging

paper clips, flags, "stickies," slips of paper or *X*'d-out 3-by-5-inch cards to mark notes

a couple of pens or pencils

a notepad to keep track of anything you may notice and want to get back to later

a companion—not necessary, but inventory goes faster and is easier if two people are involved

Manual Method

To begin, look at the first card in the shelflist for the section being inventoried. Then find the matching title on the shelf. If the shelves are in order, this process will be repeated until the section is done. It's a simple process of methodically matching the shelf card to the item on the shelf. If there are two people, one can work at the shelf and the other with the shelflist.

Ideally this back-and-forth process continues, and you zip down the shelves, item-to-shelflist, shelflist-to-item. Unfortunately, problems do crop up. You will deal with them later after you identify them. You should, however, set up a system for identifying problem materials. Perhaps you could designate a shelf on one of the book trucks or use colored stickies or 3-by-5-inch cards to identify different problems. Usually a paper clip is placed on a shelflist card to mark a missing item. See figure 5.1 for a sample problem-identification system.

When the inventory of the shelves has been completed, turn first to the items identified as missing or, more appropriately, not on the shelf. They may be in another section of the LMC; they may be checked out, on reserve, or waiting for repair. You now need to manually check through all records to see if you can account for the missing titles: regular circulation, overdue, binding, reserve, or teacher check out. As you account for an item, remove the paper clip from the shelflist. If you don't find a title, leave the paper clip and mark the shelflist card that the item is missing along with the year: "m99."

Figure 5.1   Sample System for Identifying Problems during Manual Inventory

Problem	Action
Item missing from shelf	Place a paper clip on the shelflist card
Multiple copies on shelflist	Check that all copies are present For missing copies, place a paper clip on the card and mark in pencil *m* by the appropriate copy number
Item on shelf with no shelflist card	Remove item; mark it *No Shelflist,* and place it on the book truck (Label one shelf on cart *No S.L.* to save time)
Item in poor physical condition	Remove item; place it on book truck, and identify it as *repair, replace,* or *discard* If you want to think further about the title, mark it to indicate why it was pulled: *pages missing*
Item out of order on shelf	Reshelve it If marked as possibly missing, find shelflist card and remove paper clip, then reshelve item

Automated Method

Inventory with an automated system uses the same concept as a manual one except that you scan the bar code of the item. Consequently, it's slower accounting for the titles because each item probably needs to be opened for scanning unless the bar code is on the outside. Again, if two people are working, one finds the bar code in the item, the other scans it.

Before starting an electronic inventory, check the manual for the automated system to find out what commands and preparations must be made to prepare the computer for inventory. Systems vary, and upgrades will be developed that would date any process itemized in this text. If you have a handheld scanner, the items may be scanned right at the area where they are shelved. If you have to use the same bar code wand or scanner you use at the circulation desk, you will have to remove the materials in order, cart them to the circulation terminal, scan them, then return them to the shelves. Depending on your system's configuration, as well as the proximity of electrical outlets, you may be able to take the computer to the shelves. However, carefully check out such a move to be sure there is no harm to your system. When you complete the section's inventory, the system will create a printout that will identify any problems—including missing titles—except for items with no bar codes. These you will have to pull from the shelves and identify as "no bar code."

When the automated inventory is complete, analyze the resulting printout. It will identify misshelved materials that can then be shelved correctly. It will automatically account for materials that are checked out, on reserve, or at the bindery so long as you have previously scanned them for these functions. The printout is a record of all titles the system could not account for. If you have inventoried only a portion of the collection, it may be that a title is misshelved in an area you did not inventory and you will find it later. Depending on your automation system, the item record may automatically be designated as missing during the inventory process so that patrons don't look for something that's gone. Also, depending on the system, the record may be rectified if the item is found in another section in a subsequent inventory.

The Final Step

Whichever inventory process is used, when completed it is time to deal with the items that have been pulled from the shelves and those that have been identified as missing. With an automated system, search for missing titles in obvious areas that were not in the system: for example, reserve materials that were not marked as on reserve. Once all areas are checked, create a list of missing items. Automated systems generate this as part of the process; in a manual system you must create it.

Next, clear away other items on the book trucks. If there are materials without shelflists or bar codes, first check to be sure they belong to you. Occasionally, students will place materials from other libraries into their school collection. If materials apparently belong to you, catalog and process them and get them on the shelves. If they've just "appeared" and they don't meet the criteria for adding them to the collection, discard them.

The other items on the truck—those that are in poor physical shape, unneeded duplicates, or outdated—need to be considered for action. Possibilities include discarding, donating, repairing, or replacing. Take materials for repair and rebinding off the book truck and immediately deal with them. The other decisions are part of the weeding process and are discussed in chapter 6.

INVENTORY OF OTHER MATERIAL TYPES

All materials in a collection get out of date and out of shape. All should be subjected to the same scrutiny as books. Audiovisual materials should be inventoried exactly as books are, with the same preparation, the same process, and the same analysis. The difficulty is that they will take longer because most are in containers that must be opened and checked for missing components. In addition, evaluating the age of an AV item usually means setting up equipment so it can be viewed or heard. Even if the content seems pertinent, out-of-date visuals, such as cars and clothes from decades ago, may render it useless with modern students.

Since AV materials are purchased to support the curriculum, asking teachers' assistance in evaluating an older item is a good idea. Their participation lessens the pressure on the specialist somewhat and forces teachers to notice materials they may not have known were in the collection. They may, in fact, make some good recommendations for additions.

The vertical file is a completely different inventory process. While an inventory record should exist for the subjects in the file, an accounting for each individual item probably does not. Therefore, unless everything in a folder is discarded so that the subject must be removed from the system, there's no additional record keeping. Dealing with the vertical file and periodicals is handled in chapter 6.

Upon finishing the inventory and adjusting all records, decide what reports are to be generated and with whom they are shared. At the minimum, a reporting record such as shown in figure 5.2 (see page 56) should be kept for the specialist's files. Note that equipment inventory is a separate document.

Inventory is messy work; it is tiring and perhaps frustrating. However, keep in mind all the reasons it needs to be done. Remember that organization and access are vital to your program's success. If an item can't be found, it can't be used. When inventory is completed, for whatever part of the collection you've decided, take a well-earned break and feel good about your efforts. You deserve it.

Figure 5.2   Inventory Report Form

Date: _____ Reported by: _____

Collection Area	Number of Missing Titles	Uncataloged Titles On shelf— (Missing Shelflist)	Discarded Titles	Notes
000				
100				
200				
300				
400				
500				
600				
700				
800				
900				
Biog.				
Fic				
REF				
SC				
PB				
AV				
Video				
VF				
Period.				

How does my garden grow?
Weeding and cultivating

For some reason library media specialists seem to be at split ends about weeding. Some immerse themselves in a near frenzy of "out, out, damned material," while others seem to be on a crusade to save every item unless it's falling apart. Even then they expend time, money, and energy patching and repairing. Weeding is as essential to a collection as it is to a garden. Ignore the weeds and they begin to choke out the entire collection. The flowers can no longer be seen or found; the area becomes overgrown and useless.

A collection with tacky, torn, and tired materials with sagging bindings and missing parts and with items that are yellowed or brittle with age subtly tells the patrons, "We don't care enough to provide the best for you." Students noticing the outmoded appearance get frustrated, turning to electronic sources they feel are up to date or going to another library.

Weeding can be done in one or, more typically, both of two ways: on the fly or during inventory. Weeding on the fly refers to dealing with items as you encounter them, usually at the circulation desk. Maybe something is being checked out that looks like it needs repair or replacement. Attach a note to the circulation record to look over the item when it is returned. Perhaps an item is returned and looks like it's been out since World War II. It's easy to take a moment to see if the material is in good enough shape to continue to circulate. If not, set the item aside with a note so you can later consider the options. Weeding during inventory is more concentrated and planned since at that time it is part of the process to account for the collection and keep it vital and useful.

PHYSICAL CONDITION

It's easy to remove an item that is difficult to use because of its physical condition because you can see the need to remove it and can easily convince others that it should be removed. Materials that are torn and damaged but remain on the shelf usually encourage more damage. If the outer appearance is shabby, remove the item. If parts are missing, remove it. If it's yellow or brittle from age, remove it. If there's a newer edition next to it, remove the older one. Once the uglies are off the shelf, you can look at them more carefully, considering what to do with them.

The next consideration is whether to repair or rebind. Both of these options are less desirable than they once may have been. Library media specialists used to spend time on repair because their primary function was the collection. Now, due to the many tasks specialists must perform and their vital role in instruction, repairs are either handled by volunteers or performed only on items that aren't that bad to begin with or that are very popular and unavailable for purchase. In short, repairing is not cost effective.

Rebinding is also less cost effective than it once was. If the purchase price is close to the rebinding price, it is better to buy a new copy. If a paperback version would work, there's no sense in rebinding at all, but, obviously, that depends on how much the book circulates. If it has high circulation, a paperback won't work unless it is a prebound version (a paperback book bound like a hard copy). Books to be rebound need to have a *minimum* $1/2$-inch margin on each side. The pages must be in good condition and free of marks, rips, and yellowing. If there is a newer version of the title, order it and forget rebinding.

If materials are to be rebound, they should be "checked out" to the bindery so records remain current. In a manual system, mark the check-out card "bindery" as the borrower, interfile all bindery-bound cards together, and place them in an appropriate and accessible spot.

AGE OF MATERIALS

Dated material can also provide false information that, in some cases, can be dangerous. Health care and science particularly have undergone significant changes. Certain science fair experiments contained in older books have since been found to be exceptionally harmful. For example, some older titles advocated smoking to relax nerves and ease tension. The social issues related to women, minorities, and sexually transmitted diseases such as AIDS can be hideously misleading when looked at from the perspective of ten or more years ago.

Materials that appear to be in good shape are often hard to discard, so they remain on the shelves. Sometimes library media specialists may be pressured by well-intending outsiders who think the book is sacred: if it is looks good, it is good. Principals and teachers often assume that if the copyright date is anytime after they graduated from high school, the material is OK. Principals are concerned about meeting materials standards required by accrediting agencies or, perhaps, by state law. They need to be reminded that the material may be dated if it was published before the students using it were born. Unusable materials are not worth storing.

Janitors are also self-appointed guardians of materials, frequently returning items the specialist has thrown in the garbage. Consequently, many library media specialists discard materials at home so the janitor will not bring them back or take them to the principal. The worst culprits are library media specialists who cannot part with materials. If a new edition is purchased, they keep the old one, which is as sensible as keeping the old phone book when the new one arrives. They become attached to anything on the shelves, regardless of format, believing that because it was bought, it must be worthwhile.

Materials that are outdated sometimes are passed on to other libraries. Private schools and missions become the recipients of school library media castoffs. However, if information is dated, inaccurate, and dangerous to the students in one school, it is not improved or corrected by giving it to someone else. Sometimes the effort and expense involved in giving materials to others makes it more prudent to discard them.

The decision about older materials remaining in the collection should be based on curriculum and use. If the item has not circulated for several years, it should be removed. If that prospect is too hard to handle, try to feature it in a display or find another way to encourage its use. Failing that, it's time for the discard pile. When the item is not used for any curricular area or when it is pertinent but dated, it must be removed.

OTHER WEEDING FACTORS

While age and condition may be fairly obvious criteria for weeding, there are other reasons that are somewhat related to the age of the collection. Just as information has changed over the years, so has our sensitivity and perspective. Even though we now recognize the problems associated with materials that are prejudicial, remnants may well remain on our shelves. Materials containing religious, political, sex, or race discrimination—overtly or by omission—must be evaluated.

Simply removing these materials may not be clear cut. It raises concerns about intellectual freedom and censorship that can become a quagmire, especially for a new person. Each library media specialist must read, talk, and think these issues out to form a personal philosophy that translates into action based on a policy about such issues, adopted by the school board. Such a policy is not just about weeding but about inclusion of such materials in the collection whether by retention, selection, or gifts.

Materials that appear in good shape may also be removed because of space constrictions, excessive duplication, changes in curriculum, lack of compatibility with students' reading levels, or, bluntly, poor selection. Sometimes library media specialists select by their own interests or the enthusiasm of the reviewer rather than with an objective eye toward ultimate use by their patrons. These poor selections are potential candidates for removal.

STAGES OF WEEDING

There are several stages to weeding. Identification is the first step. The next step is whether to replace the title. Again, look at the circulation—if the item is used a lot, it is obviously worth keeping in the collection. Also analyze the curriculum. If the item is part of a curricular unit, it also needs replacement. However, if neither of these factors is germane, then a more-considered judgment must be made.

When making a decision to replace an item, still other considerations come into play: price, number of similar titles, and format. If a book is removed, is a book the best replacement item, or might a videotape work better? If the price has gone up, do circulation and the curriculum demand this title? Might another one or two work better?

Still the decision to weed a title may not be easy, particularly with those that are not in disrepair and that do not contain obviously outdated material. These may be the ones that were poor choices, that just sit on the shelf, unused. One idea might be to check standard selection lists to see if the title is recommended. Another plan might be to ask teachers their opinions in these cases. Perhaps a box could be set up in the lounge that is marked "These don't check out. Should we keep them? What's your opinion?" Place pencils and small sheets of paper nearby for comments. After a couple of weeks, those items that received no support could be removed from the collection.

The most helpful tool for weeding is a weeding policy that delineates why weeding is necessary and establishes a time cycle, procedure, and criteria for removing materials. The policy should also indicate what will be done with the castoff items. For example, they may be thrown out or sent to a recycling center, put up for sale at an open house or community garage sale, or offered for free in a giveaway box in the LMC.

The policy should be well thought out and approved by the administration at the building level or, preferably, at the district level. Thus, the policy and process become more formalized . . . and more acceptable.

Once the decision is made to remove material, there are still a few more steps before the item is out of sight. First, each item must be clearly marked *discarded* so there is no assumption it was removed in error. Then the shelflist must be corrected to show when the item was removed: "D98"—discarded 1998. If the item is being replaced, that information should also be marked on the shelflist or inventory-control record when the new item arrives: "Rpl 99." If it is not to be replaced, the shelflist card and accompanying catalog cards should be removed. In an automated system the record should be purged.

THE CREW METHOD

Many practitioners use a process called the CREW method to assist in weeding their materials.[1] CREW presents formulas and specific guidelines by Dewey class to assist in removing materials. It also incorporates some catchy acronyms that quickly summarize criteria:

For Books—
  MUSTY
M—misleading
   (factually inaccurate)
U—ugly
   (beyond repair)
S—superseded (newer
   edition or better title)
T—trivial (no merit)
Y—your collection has
   no use (irrelevant)

For Audiovisual Materials—
  WORST
W—worn out
O—out of date
R—rarely used
S—system can provide
   (interlibrary loan)
T—trivial or faddish

---

1. Joseph P. Segal, *Evaluating and Weeding Collections in Small and Medium-Sized Public Libraries: The CREW Method* (Chicago: American Library Association, 1980).

WEEDING THE VERTICAL FILE
AND PERIODICALS

The vertical file is so easy to weed that it can be done at your desk or even at home. Examine each file folder, noting the condition and date of items. Discard things that are tattered, torn, or yellow. Anything older than three years (two for technology and science) should be looked over carefully. Is it historical? Is it a topic students still request? Does it relate to a subject still studied in the curriculum? Regardless of its date or condition, if the item has historical value, retain it. For example, if there are original magazine and newspaper articles from the day after John F. Kennedy's assassination, try to preserve and keep them as you would any other primary-source material. However, most older vertical file material is useless. Definitely, when a new version of a pamphlet or brochure arrives, remove the older one. A vertical file is an excellent, popular resource for students, but its value decreases dramatically as its contents age.

Periodical inventory records are not very detailed, so magazines can simply be tossed out. However, if specific issues have been entered in an automated system, or if detailed record-control cards are kept, these must be updated as issues are removed. Most library media centers have an established policy of how long they keep back issues. Nonindexed titles usually are discarded after one year; indexed titles after five years. Some centers set out the older issues for teachers to take for classroom use or clipping.

There are a few centers that inventory back issues of magazines on a regular basis so they can notify students if a requested issue is missing. This process requires a lot of time and work. Unless the magazines are the most important component of the collection and a way can be found to obtain the missing back issues, the time is usually not justified. Again, that is a decision you must make for your own situation.

If the LMC soon will become automated, weeding is extremely important. Converting from manual to automated systems is involved and costly. Neither time nor money should be spent converting materials that are outdated, useless, or in poor condition. Therefore, meticulous weeding is an essential first step for conversion to automation. If the facility is already automated, weeding remains critical to maintaining a database that is not cluttered with useless entries.

How do I keep it
all together?

Type and organization
of materials

For a long time school library media specialists dealt mainly with print materials—books, magazines, and vertical file items. This changed as the information age expanded, and the school library media center became home to a wide range of formats including all types of audiovisual items as well as computer software. The availability of so many new sources has had a dramatic impact on collection development . . . and has created a rift in the field.

ELECTRONIC VS. PRINT MEDIA

Some library media specialists believe the timeliness, access potential, speed, and vast amount of resources available in electronic media dictate expending the majority of their budgets on emerging technology, often nearly to the exclusion of print material. Their purchases center on online service, CD-ROM databases, computer software, and laser discs. They point to how quickly a book's content becomes dated and how long the publishing process takes from the moment the information is written until it finally is in published format.

On the other side are those who maintain that reading is the primary activity of the LMC program, followed by curricular research based on reading. Consequently, these advocates continue to spend their funds to build appropriate collections of the more-traditional print media. This group is bolstered by the whole-language approach, which relies less on textbooks and more on a wide range of reading materials. They also point out that, although print costs are rising, they can still purchase more print titles for the dollar than they can electronic resources.

A third perspective, that of the compromisers, sees the need for all types of resources and all types of curricular involvement. Compromisers try to balance their funds between the two types of materials. The difficulty is that electronic resources are often quite expensive and eat large chunks of the budget. Electronic resources also require expensive hardware. The units thus purchased limit the number of students who can access information at one time unless the LMC can purchase networking hardware and software—another significant expenditure. These people also understand the need for immediacy of information and the difficulty of the print format to fulfill that need.

TYPES AND HOUSING OF MATERIALS

According to recent studies, books are still the main component of most library media collections, greatly expanded by the addition of paperbacks. AV materials have undergone dramatic changes. Records, once a mainstay of the AV collection, are—or should be—gone. Audio cassette use has somewhat lessened, thanks to CD-ROMs, and filmstrips are giving way to videocassettes. Commercially prepared transparencies are being replaced by teacher-created ones. CD-ROM titles, computer software, and, for some, laser discs are entering the collection—all radically affecting collection use and development.

Periodicals are also growing in importance because their timeliness makes their content more useful for research and their brevity makes them more appealing to users. In addition, the magazine publishing field is exploding with new titles on nearly every imaginable topic. Some specialists are increasing their periodical budgets while lessening their book expenditures.

The vertical file is sort of an enigma in today's LMC. On the one hand, it is harder and harder to find inexpensive material to place in it. On the other, the temporal nature and brief format of the material, plus its ease of access and use, make it very appealing to students. Thus, many specialists rely on clippings from magazines and newspapers as well as brochures and pamphlets from governmental groups and nonprofit agencies to fill the folders.

Thus, it seems the one constant in today's materials types is their perpetual change. The one factor the library media specialist must always consider is what is best for students to succeed in the educational program.

Housing Arrangements

Not only do all these changes have an impact upon the budget but they also affect the physical set-up of the LMC. Books are relatively easy to store; after all, we've had years of experience. We move them with book carts and house them on ranges of shelves. Within each range are several sections. Each section is in order, top to bottom, before moving on to the next section. While it may be tempting to place books in order along the entire top row, from end-to-end, then the second row, and so on down, it is not practical. For one thing, it would take longer to find material than looking within one section. For another, moving books to add new arrivals is more difficult. Finally, adjusting shelf height to accommodate different sizes becomes nearly impossible.

Our one "print" housing problem may be paperbacks; we know they should be displayed face out to attract users, but we often lack the space to do it. In many collections paperbacks other than fiction are part of the regular collection, and they're shelved with the rest of the materials. It's the paperback fiction titles that we try to find some intriguing way to shelve so they'll attract readers. A number of special, space-saving units are designed for that purpose, as seen in catalogs of various library suppliers.

Current issues of periodicals are usually on open-face display shelves with periodical files used to store back issues. If popular titles are frequently stolen or vandalized, they may be kept behind the circulation desk for better control. The same principle applies to the back issues, which often are kept in a secured area if they are used extensively for research projects.

The vertical file is organized in file folders in drawers. Each folder is for a different subject. All the materials within the folder are marked with the subject so they can be returned to the correct folder after use. Some library media specialists also mark each item with a number to facilitate circulation. The number is usually the year the item was added followed by an accession number: "98-425." The folders are placed in alphabetical order in the drawers.

The AV formats have proven the most challenging to house because they do not easily fit on shelves that were designed for books. Some specialists purchase specially designed containers that are booklike in which to place AV items, and some AV producers create packaging that is booklike. With these containers, the traditional bookshelves can be used for AV materials. There are also shelving units and cabinets specially designed for AV materials. Unfortunately, many LMC budgets do not permit purchasing these. Furthermore, according to the way the LMC is used, such separate shelving may not fit within the scheme of organization.

For many years integrated shelving was *the* system to use, which meant all materials, regardless of format, were classified the same and shelved together. This posed problems: Some AV formats just didn't stay put on the shelves; they slid off the back, slipped behind other items, or ate up a lot of shelf space—a critical issue in many facilities, especially the older ones. Sometimes the items were stolen, especially video and audio cassettes and computer software.

Some LMCs with integrated shelving develop a policy permitting students to use AV materials only in the center, limiting checkout for classroom use. With this procedure the student first goes to the shelf to get the item, then to another area to get the equipment to use the item, then to a third area to set up and operate the equipment. Thus, integrated shelving is not as popular as it once was. Instead centers sometimes establish an AV area within the LMC that houses the materials and equipment. Stations are preset with equipment so the student simply gets the material and uses it. Some of these facilities do, however, place the AV materials in an area unaccessible to students. Although such procedures may curtail loss of materials, they also complicate student use and demand extra time from library media staff.

Even when we know what shelves will be used for what, we still have problems figuring out exactly where to put shelving within the LMC. Obviously, an existing center already has an established arrangement. Changing it the first year is not wise unless there is something that is totally unworkable. For example, if the paperback section is located right next to the exit, it does not take a Mensa member to figure out the location is a major factor in the number of missing items from that collection area.

Consequently, as the year progresses you should observe usage patterns, analyze how easy it is to find materials, and consider if there are any changes that would make student usage easier or better. Storing materials in the LMC should be based primarily on one concept: What is the easiest organization for students to access and use? Additional considerations that come into play besides use include the curriculum, budget, space, access to staff for assistance, vandalism, theft, and security.

ORGANIZATION OF MATERIALS

Materials in the LMC are organized in two ways: by number or by alphabet. The number system is a classification scheme wherein the numbers represent subjects so that all materials about the same subject are located in the same area. There are two number classification schemes: the Dewey Decimal system and the Library of Congress system, which actually incorporates a combination of letters and numbers. Academic libraries, some special libraries, and some large public libraries use the Library of Congress system; the vast majority of school and public libraries in the United States use the Dewey Decimal system.

The Dewey Decimal system, developed by noted librarian Melvil Dewey, is based on a series of numerical units and subunits. Determining the number to be used for a subject is discussed in chapter 10, but for now consider how the system helps organization. Materials are placed on the shelves in order by their assigned Dewey number. The numbers can become quite specific and lengthy, although many school libraries, especially at the elementary level, limit the number of digits beyond the decimal point to two or three.

Dewey Classes

The Dewey system first divides general knowledge into ten major classes:

000–099	General works
100–199	Philosophy
200–299	Religion
300–399	Social sciences
400–499	Languages
500–599	Science
600–699	Applied science
700–799	Fine arts
800–899	Literature
900–999	History

Each of these is divided into ten subclasses, which are each then further divided into ten other subclasses. For example:

900	History
910	Geography and travel
920	Biography
930	Ancient history
940	European history
950	Asian history
960	African history
970	North American history
980	South American history
990	Oceania history

After that, additional subdivision is accomplished with decimals. For example:

900	History
970	North American history
973	United States history
973.7	United States history, Civil War period
973.73	United States history, Civil War causes

Author

The Dewey number forms the top part of the call number, a number used to assign a place for the material. The call number is placed on the outside of the item so that it can be easily seen and read. The bottom portion of the call number is usually an indication of the author. (Exceptions are noted in chapter 10.) Most centers use the first three letters of the author's last name, although some use only the first letter and some use the entire last name. Thus,

973.73

Bro

is a book about the causes of the U.S. Civil War written by Joseph Brown. Other materials about the causes of the U.S. Civil War would have the same Dewey number but would have different bottom lines because of different authors. They would first be arranged by the top number, then the bottom letters. Correct order, then, would be

973.73	973.73	973.73	973.73
Bro	Gab	Gad	Mon

Other subjects assigned Dewey numbers are handled the same way, thus:

641.3	725	821.44	942	973.73	973.8	979
Bro	Bro	Bro	Bro	Bro	Bro	Bro

The difficulty in placing materials in order under this system comes when the numbers extend beyond the decimal point. For example, some individuals are not sure how to organize the following:

973.73   973.731   973.7   973.69   973.6   973.7303

The best method is to equalize the number of digits by mentally assigning *0*s to fill in the blanks, such as

973.73*00* 973.731*0* 973.7*000* 973.69*00* 973.6*000* 973.7303

It then becomes apparent the order is

973.6   973.69   973.7   973.73   973.7303   973.731

The Dewey Decimal system is used to classify all nonfiction materials including audiovisual. Maintaining one classification system makes it easier for patrons to use and for LMC staff to catalog.

Additional Collection Markings

While the Dewey Decimal system is used to classify nearly all materials, occasionally markings are added to the call number to provide additional information about the material, usually an indication of a specific collection area. For example, reference materials are marked with REF or R above the regular call number to distinguish them from the regular circulating collection. Audiovisual materials may have AV above the call number to distinguish them from print materials.

R	REF	AV
973.73	973.73	973.73
Bro	Bro	Civ

At one time audiovisual materials had a conglomeration of letters to distinguish their varied formats. In most cases, this practice has died away. If it hasn't in your center, consider eliminating it. Symbols included letter combinations like FS for filmstrip, FSS for sound filmstrip, PR for print, etc. If cataloging follows standard practice, information about the audiovisual format is within the catalog record; the patron need only read it. Designating AV call numbers is one area you need to study and make a decision based on your own situation. Personal experience has proven that the simpler, the better.

Other collection designations that indicate a separate collection area include the following:

E	picture books (easy)
SC	story collection, or SS for short stories
VF	vertical file
CAREER	career materials
or VOC	career materials
RESERVE	special materials housed behind the circulation desk or in another controlled access area

Computer Software

How the library media specialist designates and organizes computer software also may vary. Some treat it as an AV component; others create a separate special collection. Some keep it behind the circulation desk, accessible only to teachers or for in-house use, giving some sort of separate designation above its Dewey number. The software may be kept in a computer lab but be indexed in the main catalog of the LMC.

Fiction

Other letter combinations are used in a call number instead of a Dewey number to indicate different collection areas. This situation occurs when a Dewey number would be too confusing. For example, technically speaking, fiction should be in the 800s with a detailed call number that reflects language of origin and format of the item. That type of call number would make the fiction area very confusing to users. Therefore, shortcuts have been created to make access easier.

Fiction is housed separately from nonfiction and is organized alphabetically by the author's last name. The call number for all fiction, then, is the same on the top line. The bottom line again reflects the author's last name. Here are possibilities for fiction:

F	FIC	Fiction
Bro	Bro	Bro

Biographies

Biographies are handled differently from anything mentioned thus far. For one thing, the bottom line of a biography reflects not the author's name but the name of the biographee. Again, some LMCs use the first three letters of the biographee's last name, while others use the full name. The top line of a biography call number also may vary. Some LMCs use the Dewey number 921, which is the same for all individual biographies. They may shelve materials with this number in a separate area or in their natural order within the nonfiction 900s. Some use the letter B to indicate individual biographies.

However, nearly all use the number 920 for collective biographies, a single title with several biographies in it. In this case the bottom line of a 920 call number is an indication of author or title because several individuals are profiled. These 920s may be housed separately or within the 900s.

What special collection areas are created is also a local decision. Maybe there's a special collection for parents with materials on parenting, drugs, and homework help, or perhaps there is one on local history or college handbooks. Some LMCs have a professional collection for the faculty, which may or may not be housed and circulated within the general collection.

Organization of materials is of primary importance to the library media center's patrons. If they cannot find the materials, they cannot use them. If they cannot easily gain access, they become frustrated and will not return. The organization of the facility is totally up to you—and your careful review of what is best for your students and staff.

How do I know what to buy?

Selection of materials

The final decision of what items to add to the collection rests with the library media specialist. It is a heavy responsibility not to be taken lightly. It is time-consuming, complicated, and sometimes frustrating, but it is the essence of what the library media center is about. If you don't have the right materials, patrons won't come.

No matter how experienced, educated, and committed library media specialists may be, they need assistance in making intelligent decisions about the collection. They rely on several sources:

- a policy for guidance
- trusted representatives for accurate information
- experienced colleagues and cooperative teachers for advice
- respected journals and books for reviews and recommendations
- detailed knowledge of their own collection
- time to visit other facilities, conferences, and exhibits to evaluate materials first hand

SELECTION POLICY

The first thing to check before beginning selection is whether or not there is a selection policy. It may be a district document, a building policy, or one developed by the library media specialist. A selection policy establishes a recognized procedure for selection and empowers the school library media specialist to activate it. A good policy has several components:

- role and responsibility of all participants: specialist, teachers, and administrators
- philosophy of the district and the role of the library media center within that philosophy
- recommended selection procedures, including reviewing sources and personal examination
- relationship to community values and expectations
- criteria for selecting materials, including formats, needs, and relation to curriculum
- handling of complaints about materials
- handling of gifts
- removal of materials (weeding)
- incorporation of the principles of intellectual freedom, evidenced by inclusion of the Library Bill of Rights (see appendix F for an explanation)

If a policy does not exist, it should be created, preferably at the district level. In the meantime, selection should go forward.

THE COLLECTION

As with so many other aspects of the new job, selection is yet another task that cannot be effectively started until you know what is already in the collection. There is no reason to buy until you're fully aware of what you already have. Therefore you probably will not undertake selection for the first two to three months. Unfortunately, because most school budgets require nearly complete budget expenditure before a target date, usually in early spring, selection will have to be activated by the end of

December unless your predecessor spent the allotted funds for the year. (See chapter 14 for details on the budget.)

If you haven't been able to conduct a quick inventory of the collection, start browsing the shelves. Get a sense of the titles that are there; look over the AV materials; check circulation records. Gather statistics on the collection, using whatever past records you can find.

How many titles do you have in each area of the collection?

What's the average age of the materials in each area?

What areas seem to have the largest concentration of titles?

How does that match with the curricular units?

Do the reading levels seem appropriate?

Look over purchase orders for the last two years. What areas of the collection were enhanced? By how many titles? With how much money?

One way to get a quick sense of the date of a collection is by analysis. Some automated systems have a procedure wherein you can get the average dates for a particular area. Check the manual or call the vendor for your system. You can also analyze a printout of the shelflist for collection areas. If there's no automation, conduct an analysis with the shelflist. Write down the copyright date of every tenth or fifteenth title. Add up all the dates, divide by the number of entries and, voilà, you have an average date for whatever area you've analyzed.

Another technique to use in analyzing what's already in the collection is to check against recommended selection guides. Several companies publish these, and at least one is probably in the professional or reference collection. Simply check the titles listed against the ones owned, but remember many standard selection sources have somewhat dated recommendations. Alternatively, find the lists of recommended titles produced yearly by various associations, such as the American Library Association, and compare them with what's on the shelves. Some reviewing periodicals also create compilations of reviews that are available in print or CD-ROM format.

All the suggestions given so far are time-consuming. As a new person on the job, you are probably knee-deep in trying to keep up with everything else that's going on. How, then, you wonder, could you possibly do all this analyzing of the collection? The parts that involve interaction with teachers *should* be done by you not only to find out about the collection but also to assume the role of instructional consultant to the teachers. When it comes to checking titles against sources or computing copyright dates, you don't need personal involvement; you merely need the results. For that you can use volunteers, clerks, or trusted students.

If the entire selection process is still too overwhelming the first year, concentrate on smaller areas, such as reference, periodicals, and audiovisual material. It would take far less time to evaluate what's available in these areas. In addition, purchases targeted in smaller areas make a more-noticeable impact. Just be sure not to neglect any specific teacher requests for other areas.

EVALUATIVE TECHNIQUES

There are a number of ways to facilitate the evaluative process. Some involve people's opinions; some rely on authorities; probably a combination of techniques is best.

Staff and Student Assistance

Consistently involve staff members in selection. Watch carefully what teachers check out. Meet with grade levels or departments and find out what their primary units will be for the year. Ask teachers what they feel needs to be added. Ask them what they've missed in previous years. As you get a sense of what is being studied and what is desired, check to see what is in the collection and how up to date it is, then share this information with the staff.

When you find a title you think will be appropriate for the collection, ask teachers from that subject area what they think. Show them reviews or publishers' catalogs. If you are able to obtain a copy for preview, ask them to look it over. Even if teachers decline because of a time pinch, they will appreciate your efforts to include them.

Students are frequently overlooked as partners in selection, which is ironic since their use is supposedly our primary concern. Students' opinions can be solicited through a variety of ways:

- developing an on-site exhibit
- providing a suggestion box for their exclusive use
- offering review magazines or publishers' catalogs in a special area with order cards
- creating a student club or choosing selected groups of students

Personal Evaluation

The best way to evaluate any item is by personal examination. Many school library media conferences, at both the state and the national levels, feature exhibitors who have materials on hand to be examined up close and personal. Often a separate exhibit is filled with materials from assorted publishers. Sometimes publishers will send you examination copies or territory representatives will bring them to your LMC.

If you cannot attend such conferences or make contacts with the appropriate publishers, it's time to go on the road. Visit school and public libraries in the area. Look over their collections. See what items they have purchased and preview them on site at the library. Talk to the librarians and find out what they recommend.

You can also visit bookstores. Many chains have large stores with large collections and comfy preview areas. It's a great way to spend a morning, afternoon, or evening. Everything is organized by subjects, and it's all new.

Sources for Reviewing

Many school library media specialists rely on reviews in professional periodicals to help them make decisions about purchases. While such sources may bring titles to your attention, they should not be relied upon exclusively. First of all, they only review about 25 percent of the materials published. Second, they review few small-press releases. Finally, in some periodicals, the reviewers are practitioners who are as expert in analyzing materials as you are; in others, the reviewers may know how to analyze the material for accuracy, writing quality, material quality, etc., but they cannot know the curriculum and students of your school the way you do. Therefore, reviews are one source but not *the* source for selection.

Publishers and Distributors

Once you become accustomed to purchasing, or as you grow familiar with materials you find particularly useful, you'll begin to find publishers whose material is consistently well done and accurate, material you can count on. Without further evaluation you may feel at ease purchasing items featured in these publishers' catalogs. Some publishers or distributors may have representatives who travel the area. After you build up a good rapport with the representatives, you will determine which are honest with you about their products. You'll be able to trust their advice and rely on their judgment; they become another source for your selection.

See appendix G for a list of companies who've actively supported the school library media profession through their involvement with AASL. These are reliable sources to begin with as you establish rapport with companies as part of the selection process.

CRITERIA

When deciding what to purchase for the collection there are a lot of variables to keep in mind regarding the item's content and physical format. Content considerations include

- relation to the curriculum, existing collection, and community values
- accuracy and validity
- appropriateness to students' reading ability
- needs expressed by students and staff

Other than content issues, you need to consider each item for the following:

- material type
- durability
- organization and presentation
- appeal to students
- quality of style and any illustrations
- producer's or publisher's reliability
- cost
- ownership compared with interlibrary loan

To better understand these factors, a few examples may help. Let's say you are considering an expensive laser disc requested by the science department, but for the same amount of money you can add several titles for a research unit for the English department and some books requested by students. As another example, perhaps you are asked to buy a title that you have personally examined and that you know will not hold up for more than three circulations because of its flimsy binding or an audiovisual kit from a publisher identified in the professional literature as being unreliable and frequently inaccurate. These circumstances demonstrate issues that need to be resolved in a professional manner that incorporates the other factors in selection. No single criterion should be used for an addition to the collection.

SAVING SOME DOLLARS

Some methods can save precious library media dollars. These are listed in the next sections, but any of them need to be considered in full light of established selection procedures and policies of the individual LMC.

Gifts

Donations to the school library media center are usually well-intended but are not always worthwhile additions. First, dealing with gifts should be part of the selection policy. Second, gifts should be evaluated under the same criteria as purchases.

Finally, gift givers should realize that their donations will not automatically be added to the collection but will be handled the same as purchases.

Gifts can sometimes be a generous and helpful boost to the collection. Schools have received computer hardware and software, TV studios and equipment, valuable research periodicals, and sets of pertinent titles. They have also been the recipients of people's garage and attic cleaning, receiving things so outdated or in such poor condition that no one else wanted them. To avoid hurt feelings and angry phone calls to the principal, be sure a gift policy is in place—one that's been approved by the principal or, preferably, by the board of education. It's especially important that the policy address the issue of equipment. Computers and accompanying hardware that are too far behind the times for the consumer are not necessarily a great addition to the school. Such equipment must fit within the parameters the school has established and the program the school has designed, and that fact must be apparent to the giver. In general, if you wouldn't buy the gift offered, don't accept it.

Periodicals

At one time, elementary LMCs purchased periodicals primarily to teach and encourage reading. The development of both periodical indexes and research-oriented magazines geared to younger students opened up research possibilities. Conversely, at the secondary level, new titles are constantly being introduced that appeal to the varied tastes and interests of adolescents. However, due to budgetary constraints, some library media specialists at the secondary level do not purchase periodical titles unless they are included in standard indexing sources, such as *Readers' Guide to Periodical Literature*. Research periodicals available on CD-ROM or microform with an accompanying index are also being used by some specialists to replace paper format and to lower periodical costs. In some instances, specialists do not purchase specialized titles they can easily obtain through interlibrary loan. These decisions are greatly influenced by circulation and available funding.

Cooperative Collection Development

To pool resources and save money, libraries are developing consortia to cooperatively purchase materials that they can share. The primary areas for such cooperative efforts are periodicals, reference, and special collections. Normally, the libraries subscribe to a set list of titles with one library purchasing periodicals in a specific subject area or title and another agreeing to purchase a different subject or title. Obviously, each facility purchases frequently requested titles, and cooperative efforts are employed for lesser-used titles.

Library systems may maintain a database of all periodical holdings of member libraries—schools, public, and academic. Not only is this holdings list an excellent source for sharing, it is also a way to preview periodical titles. The list is especially helpful for research because copies of articles from periodicals the LMC does not own can be obtained for student use.

Interlibrary Loan

Many regional or state library systems have a database, available online or on CD-ROM, for interlibrary loans of books and other circulating items. A title may be identified, requested, and circulated online—if your LMC is part of the system. In some states the requested material may be sent to a local public library, a systems headquarters, or directly to your school district. Checking with your local or state public library about what is available in your area and how to become part of it is an excellent way to obtain materials that may be beyond your purchase capabilities. Investigate the exact procedure, expectations of your role, costs (if any), and time lines to determine if the process is helpful. Students and teachers are very impressed when they receive a title from a university or a library in another state, thanks to your efforts.

ONGOING EFFORTS

One way to become more adept at selection is to be constantly prepared for it. Keep order cards with you whenever you read professional titles. Carry some with you when you visit other facilities or conferences or attend meetings with teachers. Write one out for every item you see that appears to be good for the collection. You have a standardized form you can then file in a drawer or box by subject area. This becomes your "want" list. It will never be empty or used up. There will always be priorities, usually limited by budget, that will force choices. However, you never know when someone will come up with some grant money for some isolated area, and you will be ready with some potential items, in spite of tight time lines.

When you finally get comfortable with selection, it becomes part of you at all times. You'll be browsing a shop on vacation and notice something that's perfect for the collection. You'll be reading the newspaper and spot a clipping or drawing that would work well for the vertical file. You'll be watching TV and see an ad or hear a news segment on a new item that will help a teacher with a unit you were recently discussing. All that just means you've arrived as a library media specialist!

9

How do I keep track of everything?

Circulation

Being responsible for the collection includes managing who uses it, under what circumstances, and with what consequences if there is misuse. It often also involves keeping statistics about circulation to evaluate collection use. As with most procedures, there are two possibilities for circulation systems: automated and manual.

In an automated system, loan periods are set up within the computer when the system is activated but may be changed if necessary. Bar codes are used for both items and patrons, and both check-out and check-in consist of scanning the bar codes into the system. The computer then stores the record, tracks its status, assigns the item to the patron's record, and keeps whatever information is necessary to later generate statistical records. The computer even keeps track of the overdues, blocking subsequent check-out attempts. Some automation systems include a process wherein a check-out may be blocked because of a message the specialist places on the patron record, such as a reminder that an item "on hold" has come in. The only manual process is the placing or marking of a date due notice in the item as a reminder for the patron.

In a manual system the library media staff monitors the check-out to see that the proper information is given by the patron, stamps the date due on the borrower's card and the item, stores the borrower's card in a predetermined manner, keeps track of the item's status, and completes whatever information is necessary for circulation statistics.

Some library media centers, especially small ones or those at the elementary level, use an honor system for check-out to save staff time. Students simply fill out the borrower's card with the required information and place it in a box or tray clearly identified for the day's check-outs.

PATRONS

Obviously, a school library media center's primary users are students and staff. But staff has often meant only teachers; it should mean everyone employed within the school. It's amazing what PR bonuses can be accomplished by encouraging secretaries and custodians to use the LMC. The principal should understand that usage privileges are also extended to administrators. Another group school library media centers have just begun to consider is parents. Some school LMCs even establish a special "parenting" collection for their parents.

MATERIALS AND CIRCULATION PERIODS

The first circulation decision is what items may be checked out and for how long. If the parameters already in place seem reasonable, continue them. However, it is still a good idea to review the policy and procedure.

Today's LMC has a more open attitude than in the past; consequently, nearly everything circulates. However, items that need to be available on a daily basis have more-limited circulation periods so that they are available to patrons throughout the day. Among these limited circulation materials are reference books, current magazines, some AV materials, and reserve materials for a specific project or teacher. Some facilities deny circulation of AV materials, magazines, and reference materials. Circulation is also influenced by the size of the collection: the more materials, the more liberal the circulation time.

Some LMCs limit the number of items a student may check out, especially for younger students who are just learning the responsibility of being a borrower. Others may place a limit on the number of a certain type of material. For example, the LMC policy may state a student may borrow five items, but it also states that only one videocassette is allowed, only three magazines, etc. The limits on the type of items override the limit on total numbers of items.

The circulation period depends not only on the item but also on the patron, including how many patrons and items there are. Fewer items and more patrons lead to more restrictive circulation periods so that materials may be more accessible to all. Teachers usually have a longer circulation period than students, but the practice of checking items out to them for a year or even a semester at a time needs to be seriously examined. If a teacher needs an item for that long, perhaps he or she should purchase it from the budget for the room so the LMC copy is available to everyone. Older students usually get longer circulation periods than younger ones. Students who have proven themselves irresponsible may receive circulation limits. And special patrons— student teachers, parents—may be on a case-by-case basis.

Other factors influence loan time. The standard junior and senior high school loan time for books has been two weeks with a one-time, two-week renewal. However, constant renewals and losses of materials have led some specialists to experiment with loan periods. Consequently, many high schools allow students a one-month loan with a one-time, two-week renewal. Elementary students frequently have a one-week loan with a one-week renewal. This time period coincides with scheduled class visits to the LMC in schools with a regularly scheduled program.

High-use materials usually circulate overnight, frequently from after school until the first hour of the next school day. These materials include reference items, AV materials, current periodicals, and reserves. Other materials may have different circulation times, such as back issues of magazines and vertical file materials for one week. AV materials may vary according to their format: one week for most AV materials and overnight for videotapes. The loan period for different material types depends on the individual LMC situation, but varied circulation periods are recommended.

Date Due

One problem library media specialists have dealt with is the day items should be due. The past practice has been that the item is due one week or two weeks (or whatever) from the date it was checked out. Thus, there are materials due—and overdue— every school day. The record keeping becomes involved, to say the least. Some schools have all regular circulating materials due on the same *day* of the week, thus considerably cutting down on daily work. In other words, overdues for regularly circulating materials are done weekly rather than daily.

The obvious problem with this system is that someone who checks an item out a day or two before the selected day of the week gets a shorter circulation period. However, since the day of the week applies only to the regular circulation period of two weeks or one month, the shortage is not significant. Students quickly learn the system, adapting check-out to their maximum benefit. While this concept may sound complicated, it saves clerical time on overdues and check-ins.

CHECK-OUT

Students and staff need a designated procedure to check out items. With automated systems, the procedure simply involves presenting a valid library ID card. Because teachers often don't carry their cards with them, a file with teachers' names and bar codes can be kept at the circulation desk. In a manual system, borrowers sign the card included within the item. Borrowers other than students may use a special indication after their names (*F* for faculty, *P* for parent) so the specialist knows which patron file to search to send overdue notices. A sign should be posted at the circulation desk to remind patrons of these procedures.

The specialist decides what information is needed from each borrower for the patron registration file. For example:

Teachers	Full name and department or grade level
Other staff	Full name, department or position, and phone number
Parents	Full name, phone number, and address

A registration file for students usually consists of their class schedules. In the elementary grades, the student's name on the card, followed by a designation of contact teacher, may be sufficient, eliminating the need for any separate registration file.

A standard borrower's card, available from any library supply company, is used for check-out. (See figure 9.1.) Some facilities use different colors or types of cards to distinguish between types of materials or loan periods. For example:

books	white cards	1 month	white cards
AV	blue cards	1 week	blue cards
magazines	green cards	overnight	green cards

Date-due slips or cards, also available from library suppliers, are placed on the item. The date due is both a reminder to the patron and a part of the check-in system.

If students do not finish with material during the allotted circulation period, they may wish to extend their time. Renewing material is a relatively simple process. The student brings the item to the center, the card is marked "Renew" beneath the student's name, a new date due that coincides with the renewal term is stamped on the item and the card, and the student has an extended time slot. In automation, the item is simply scanned and *renew* is selected as the option. If a student renews without bringing in the item, the material isn't marked; therefore, a visible reminder of due date is not on the item, which could create check-in problems.

CIRCULATION MANAGEMENT

Once the patron has borrowed an item, it is the library media staff's duty to keep track of the loan. (Automation does this for you.) Most commonly, the circulation desk has a series of trays that will hold the standard 3-by-5-inch borrowers' cards. Charging tray guides divide the trays into sections by date, teacher

Figure 9.1   Book Pocket, Circulation Card, and Date Due Form

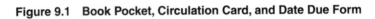

917.2 T	Trevino, Elizabeth Borton. Here is Mexico	

DATE DUE	BORROWER'S NAME	ROOM NUMBER

917.2   Trevino, Elizabeth Borton.
T   Here is Mexico.

School Name

and Address

DATE DUE

name, item type, or whatever you set up. Cards for materials checked out that day are kept at the front of one of the trays in no particular order.

At the end of the school day all cards for items circulated that day are sorted and placed in the appropriate tray under the date due. Usually the cards are put in alphabetical order by author (or title if there's no author), but some library media specialists separate the materials into types. For example, the first group filed behind the appropriate date due may be nonfiction items in order by Dewey number, followed by fiction and short stories in author alphabetical order, followed by AV material in numerical order, followed by periodicals and vertical file alphabetically by title or subject. This type of system, however, requires switching back and forth between numbers and letters and can be confusing to clerks, volunteers, or student aides who may have to work with it. Using just the alphabet seems to work fine, perhaps dividing the cards into books, AV, and other. Again, the decision is based on what works for you and your staff.

A technique used in LMCs that have scheduled classes incorporates all borrowers' cards for one class together in a packet that is usually held with a rubber band and placed under either the date due or the teacher's name.

CHECK-IN

The circulation desk staff is responsible for checking in returned items and getting them ready to return to the shelves. In an automated system, it's a simple scanning process. In a manual system, it involves matching the correct borrower's card with the item. The process is relatively simple: look at the item to determine the date due, then search in the appropriate tray under the due date for the matching card. Remove the card from the tray, place it in the item, and set the item aside to be returned to the shelves.

Unfortunately, some individuals who are responsible for checking in materials get too hasty and grab the wrong card, creating endless nightmares for borrowers and staff alike. Anyone working at check-in should be trained and cautioned to be very careful about the process. Multiple copies, authors with more than one work, authors with the same last name, call numbers that are the same but for different items—all these can create a mix-up. If items have accession numbers, these should also be on the borrower's card and serve as a check. Multiple copies should have copy numbers on the item and on the card so that these can be matched.

OVERDUES

The most time-consuming, frustrating part of circulation is overdue materials. Keeping track of overdue materials and getting
them back is the curse of the library media staff. The problem
seems to be constantly on the increase as students think less
about what others' needs may be and more about themselves.
Library media specialists nearly exhaust themselves trying to get
students to return materials promptly. They also try a variety of
gimmicks to extend overdues and entice students to return materials: fines, no fines, "grace" periods, detentions, loss of check-
out privileges, and letters and calls to parents. There is no cure-
all, no answer that eliminates the problem. It's best to accept
overdues as a necessary evil of loaning materials and plow away
at trying to get them returned.

The first step, naturally, is to remind patrons when materials
are due. The date due card, slip, or stamp on the item is part of
this reminder. Some specialists also keep a date due sign at the
desk or exit:

Materials checked out today are due on _____

The next step is to notify patrons when materials become
overdue, usually by sending reminders. Overdue notices usually
are sent weekly except for overnight materials. How students
are notified depends on your system, but accept in advance that
a few students will be notified over and over and over.

An automated system generates the overdue list in whatever
order and format you request. You follow up by sending notices
for each student to whatever room or teacher has been designated as the contact. Sometimes individual notices are sent,
sometimes designated teachers receive a list of the students in
their classes who have overdues. Individual notices usually get
a better response from students, but many teachers resent the
time for distribution (unless it's a homeroom with the purpose of
student contact). It is hoped the teachers will then pressure the
students into returning the items. At the elementary level, that
hope is usually fulfilled. At the higher levels, the teacher posts
the lists or passes out the slips, letting students handle their own
responsibilities. Titles of items should be included only on notices that are individually distributed, not on those that are

posted. Overdue notices can be created locally or purchased from library suppliers. (See figure 9.2.)

Most library media specialists establish a fairly elaborate process of accelerated notices for students who do not respond to the first one. Each additional notice is another "step" in a process of increasing penalties or threats. Ultimately the parents

Figure 9.2   Overdue Notice Forms

OVERDUE

The following library materials checked-out to you are overdue. Please return them promptly.

Card Number:_____

_____

_____

_____

_____

Reorder # 46125

DID YOU FORGET ?

Our records show the library materials you borrowed are now overdue. Please return them promptly. Thank you.

Card Number:_____

_____

_____

_____

_____

Reorder # 46123

Source: Highsmith, Inc., 1997. Further reproduction without written permission is strictly prohibited.

and/or the school disciplinarian get involved in helping to resolve the problem. To some, that may seem an overreaction, but
on principle, an item kept in one student's possession is thereby
denied to others. The problem becomes more severe if the item
is costly, popular, or required for a particular project.

Material circulated on an overnight basis cannot wait a week
before action is taken for its return; it needs to be checked and
followed up daily. The best way, even though it is time-
consuming, is to seek out the student. Get a copy of all students'
schedules for the LMC. When an overnight item isn't returned,
look up the student's schedule, go to the room, ask to see the
student, and inquire about the material. If necessary, go to the
locker with the youngster and get the item. If the problem continues with the same student, who may be merely using you to
return the item rather than bringing it back, exact a penalty from
the student to correct the behavior.

When material is overdue, create an overdue list for the use
of library media staff. As items are returned, mark the list so that
it is kept current. Then, when the next overdue list is generated
(in a manual system) the older records do not need to be
relisted.

It is wise to have a school level policy about fines, overdues,
and lost materials; it is far better to have a district policy. Not
only does a policy lend administrative support, it also alerts the
administration to the nature of the problem and lets them make
some decisions regarding the consequences. It is also easier to
work with parents when the school board, or at least the administration, has agreed this is a problem that merits some attention.

Fines and Penalties

For some time there has been controversy over fines. Some ve-
hemently oppose them, feeling they generate poor PR for the
center and punish only the youngsters who are poor. Others advocate them because it's the same type of system students will
face in academic or public libraries. Advocates further justify
fines by indicating that the fines collected are used to buy extra
items for the center so the students are, in effect, assisting the

program. Personal experience shows fines rarely work unless they are for significant amounts. Most students today, especially above the middle school level, are not bothered by a 10 cent per day penalty. However, if fines are levied, one factor that must be considered is a schedule of maximum fines so that no one ends up owing more in fines than the material is worth.

There should be some consequence for denying others the use of materials, even if it isn't monetary. Although most students don't like having their parents notified, and most parents don't appreciate it either, it usually gets results. (See figure 9.3 for a sample parental notification letter.) Students should not be assigned detention, however, or have privileges suspended without parent notification. While sending a letter may be the least confrontational (and can be handled by a clerk or volunteer, saving time), a phone call has the most impact and costs the least. With so many parents working today, it's hard to reach them at home. Messages left on machines have the same problem as letters—the student can reach them first and eliminate them so Mom or Dad never knows. A call at work is disruptive and embarrassing to the parent. Although it may create ill will toward us, it also gets results and should be kept in mind as a last resort.

Students also do not like being called in by a member of the administration to discuss the problem. Members of the administration may feel they have more important things to do than take care of what should be the library media specialist's job. Both viewpoints demonstrate the library media specialist's dilemma. Because we do not have a regular contact with students, including grading them, we lack a certain amount of contact with and control over them. When we enlist the assistance of others, we impose on them and add to their duties. Therefore, we need to examine what we can do within our own facility to encourage returns.

One thing we can do is to suspend privileges. After materials are overdue for a certain length of time, we can revoke a student's borrowing privileges. With an automated system, this is easily accomplished by setting an overdue block in the system. With a manual system, we need to establish a list that every person at the circulation desk must check religiously. The one situation we must avoid is denying students the right of coming into

Figure 9.3   Sample Letter to Parents about Overdue Material

Date _____

Dear parents of _____

The reading of library books is basic; it is also a privilege. Your student's library check-out privileges have been temporarily discontinued because the following materials have been overdue or lost for two months. Several reminders have been given to the student.

Material	Amount Due
_____ book/books	$_____
_____ magazine	$_____
_____ vertical file item	$_____
_____ audiovisual item	$_____

Would you please assist in locating the lost materials or paying the replacement cost? We regret that the student will not be able to check-out materials from the library media center until this problem is resolved.

Please call _____ if we can be of assistance.

Sincerely,

Library Media Specialist

School Principal

Source: Courtesy of Library Media Services Department, Raytown C-2 School District, Raytown, Missouri.

the center with their classes. However, we can deny them check-out privileges and, if necessary, LMC use before and after school, for study hall, or in any situation not involving a class.

If restricting borrowing does not resolve the problem, we can extend the curtailment. School library media centers have won the cooperation of their administrations in restricting students' activities. In some schools, graduating seniors are not issued caps and gowns until they fulfill all school obligations, including rectifying overdues. In others, student activities may be curtailed, semester examinations may have to be taken under different circumstances, and library obligations may be added to semester registration fees. All these possibilities need to be explored for administrative support and legal implications.

Another possibility is student detention—but not the usual type. Many detentions are served after school or on Saturday mornings under supervision of the administrators. The students study, read, or sleep, simply marking time. They don't like it, but it's not a major problem for them. A better tactic is to have detentions before or after school (students have the option) that involve work, not just passing time. Students can shelve books, read shelves, refile materials, or clean shelves. They do not like performing these tasks, but it may be a far, far better thing that they do than paying fines.

Yet another option to bear in mind when dealing with overdues is an appeal to the faculty. Sometimes they have no idea what we're dealing with, how frustrating it gets, or what impact it has on the program and the resources they need. Asking the principal for a five-minute spot at a faculty meeting to appeal for their assistance may be very helpful—but it can't be done frequently. Asking not only for teachers' cooperation but for their ideas may yield some new technique you've never thought of that can be very helpful.

It is entirely possible that there may be legitimate reasons for a student's material being overdue. Maybe they were sick, or there was a family emergency or a disaster of some type. If a student brings in such an excuse, give him or her the opportunity to prove it. A note from the school nurse or the doctor, a newspaper clipping or police report—something concrete and that was not produced by the student or parent may verify the tragedy and should wipe out the fine. Remember, some students can and will create extravagant stories to avoid consequences, especially if they don't have to prove them.

Damaged and Lost Materials

Occasionally, students will lose or damage materials. This is a bad situation because it makes a collection item unavailable to

other students. If it's a problem beyond the student's control—
that can be proved—waive the obligation. For example, there
may have been a car accident, a house fire, or a tornado, but
those instances are rare. More often it is student neglect or indifference, so they must pay for the damage or replacement.

If an item is damaged beyond repair, the student pays for a
new one. Damage assessments should be according to a standard formula figured out by the library media staff and adopted
by the administration. Most LMCs also assess a processing or ordering fee for a replacement to cover shipping, cataloging, and
processing costs. The usual price is the replacement value of the
item plus one or two dollars. If an item is out of print or unavailable, a standard fee is adopted. Parents should be notified
if a student is being charged for loss or damage.

If a student doesn't report an item as being lost, some facilities set a time limit, then declare it lost. At that point the student
must pay for the item. If he or she doesn't pay, the types of
penalties listed previously are invoked. If an item is found and
returned, the student is reimbursed for whatever was paid minus
the fines incurred up to the date the item was declared lost.

It is wise to keep good records of student payments. Use a
receipt book that has either carbons or NCR paper. That way the
student gets a receipt and the LMC keeps a record. Each transaction should include the date, student's name, amount paid,
fees assessed, and name of the item involved. It might be wise
to include the fine that would have been levied if the item had
been overdue. Then if the item is returned, the fees can be returned less the fines. An automated system contains a process
for recording fees levied and paid.

Student Claims

On occasion students claim they have not checked out an item,
or they have already returned it. In the former case, the borrower's card can be pulled to review the student's signature, or
the record can be pulled up on automation and the student ID
examined. Chances are the student either checked it out or allowed someone else to use his or her ID card, in which case the
student is still responsible. To check accuracy in an automated

system, scan the student ID to be sure the proper name is connected with it in the system. A forged signature, only a problem with manual systems, is a different story that probably involves the administration.

When a student claims to have returned an item, the best course is to walk to the appropriate shelf area with the student and look for the item together. If it's there, apologize and clear all charges, even if you suspect the student planted it. The important thing is that the item is back. If it is not, point out the problem to the student and indicate he or she is still responsible.

SECURITY SYSTEMS

In a sense, security systems are part of the circulation process because they block removal of materials unless they go through the circulation system. Part of the check-out process is to deactivate the security device in an item so that materials can be legitimately removed from the LMC. Part of the check-in process is to reactivate that same device.

If your LMC has a security system that functions well, be grateful. If not, and your inventory shows high loss figures, start planning your strategy, courting your allies (administration, businesses, and the PTO/PTA), and counting your pennies so you can purchase one. Security systems are expensive, and it takes a lot of time to place security devices in all circulating items—which students frequently find and remove. Security systems may be beaten by savvy students, but that doesn't negate their assistance in curtailing loss.

CIRCULATION STATISTICS

Many school library media specialists keep circulation statistics. Again, an automated system can be set up to generate these figures at predetermined intervals. In a manual system, the staff must calculate the figures. Each day all the borrowers' cards are tallied, usually by categories and type of borrower. These figures are then added up each week, then each month. The figures could be used to evaluate collection usage and to demonstrate usage patterns to the administration. See figure 9.4 for a form that is available to help gather the information.

CONFIDENTIALITY

An issue that has come up in recent years is the confidentiality of student circulation records. Legal sources claim that the name of the borrower and the items borrowed should not be a matter of public record, nor should anyone be able to easily discover that information. Automation systems control this problem because the records are available only to staff, and specifics can be purged from patrons' records. However, over-due lists generated by an automated system usually list the patron's name in conjunction with a specific title; therefore, some centers generate name only lists.

In manual systems, the student's name is on a borrower's card that can be viewed by subsequent borrowers or any other interested party for as long as the card lasts. In an attempt to maintain confidentiality, some LMCs block out the borrower's name when the item is returned, using a thick black marker. It usually obliterates the name, and it definitely indicates the library media staff is attempting to maintain confidentiality.

The circulation desk is the busiest area of the center. Not only does everyone come there to check materials in and out, they also come there to ask questions and to check on the status of materials. It is also the area where angry people will come to protest what they consider to be unfair overdues or other problems. They will be irate with whomever is behind the desk because they are angry with the system and the process. Therefore, the first person they encounter represents, to them, that system and that process. Consequently, the circulation desk is where the best staff members must work, the ones most able to be objective, to remain calm, and to project a positive image. Established procedures and forms will give staff members the support they need to encounter patrons.

Figure 9.4 Circulation Statistics Form

Daily Record

Date ....

Circulation	
General Works	000
Philosophy	100
Religion	200
Social Sciences	300
Language	400
Pure Science	500
Applied Science	600
Arts, Recreation	700
Literature	800
History	900-909 930-999
Travel	910-919
Biography	B920
Periodicals	
Vertical File Material	
Total Non-Fiction	
Fiction	
Grand Total	

Signature
(OVER)

HIGHSMITH #46-206   PRINTED IN U.S.A.

OTHER MATERIALS

Clippings	
Films	
Pictures	
Film Strips	
Phone Records	
Music	
Maps	
Documents	
Other	

STATISTICS

Reserve Cards Mailed	
Overdue Cards Mailed	
Books Mended	
Books Discarded	
Other	

Source: Courtesy of Highsmith, Inc., 1997. Further reproduction without permission is strictly prohibited.

10

What do all those letters and numbers mean?

Classifying, cataloging, and processing

Back in the dark ages, when I was a novice in the field, I was taught that cataloging was the technical aspect of the profession. My intimate knowledge of Dewey and Cutter separated me from others, making me unique. My "gift" of knowing how to put numbers and letters together to organize materials, my ability to consistently create catalog cards that had the right information in exactly the right place every time, my care in stamping "secret pages"—these were the things that invoked a respect for my place in the program. I remember, painfully, my shame when my practice catalog cards were returned with red circles drawn where I had added in or left out a space, a comma, a period, or a semicolon. I lived in fear that this is how I would spend endless days in my new job.

When I got out into the real world I found that the specialist's role was changing, and even though cataloging was important, there were far more exciting things I could do that were part of my job. It was very tempting, and very easy, to ignore the cataloging and processing. Because the answers to student and staff information needs might be locked up in the very items that were lingering on the back shelves, I reluctantly dealt with the intricate details of original cataloging and processing.

Then came preprocessing—classifying, cataloging, and processing done by book jobbers and other companies as an option when buying materials from them. This option saved tremendous amounts of time and could be matched to the procedures used in most LMCs. Granted, everything had to be checked over and minor adjustments made to match each library media center's idiosyncrasies. Compared with original cataloging, the time required was minimal. Materials were ready for patrons, leaving me with time to tend to other aspects of being a library media specialist.

Then came automation, and everything dramatically changed. Card catalogs and the mounds of 3-by-5-inch cards in them became an endangered species, kept alive in isolated facilities that were philosophically or financially unable to make the transition. With automation came renewed recognition of the importance of standardization in the field. Interlibrary loan and database sharing through computers developed with a speed and wealth of resources beyond anything we'd ever imagined.

Computers were fussy; records for materials had to match exactly to get what a patron requested on interlibrary loan. What made those records match was a standardized way of entering bibliographic information: MARC (MAchine Readable Cataloging) became the rule for everyone—regardless of the type of catalog used in a center. So whether your center uses the "old" card catalog or an automated system, whether you create catalog cards originally, buy them from commercial sources, or don't use them at all because of automation, MARC should be the basis for your cataloging of materials.

Before entering the detail-specific world of MARC, however, first consider what's involved in getting an item from the carton in which it arrives to the shelves where users can find it. After it's been checked in (covered in chapter 13), there remain several steps:

1. *classifying*—assigning the numbers or letters that form a call number indicating the subject that determines placement on the shelves

2. *cataloging and filing*—preparing a record for each item so that patrons can access it through an index, whether a card or an electronic catalog

3. *processing*—physical preparation of borrowers' cards, call number markings, etc., so that the item can be located and checked out

CLASSIFICATION

Classifying was discussed briefly in chapter 7 to provide a sense of how things are organized on the shelves. Checking that chapter will reacquaint you with the numbers and letters that are assigned for various collection items. The key source for assigning those "magical" numbers is the *Dewey Decimal Classification and Relative Index* that comes in both an abridged and unabridged version. The Library of Congress classification system also has a guide for assigning categories, but this system is not used in most school library media centers.

Dewey System

For most LMCs, the abridged version of Dewey is adequate, but some larger centers with larger collections prefer the unabridged because it is more specific. Both guides contain tables and explanations of Dewey numbers with a subject index to assist in finding the right number. Learning to use the *Dewey Index* is not that difficult, but it is best to take a cataloging class so that minimum confusion ensues. These classes are available from any institution that offers a library degree, as well as from many community colleges.

Suggested Dewey numbers for materials are also available in a number of other sources. Many material selection guides include suggested Dewey numbers as part of the information about a recommended item. So do some reviewing sources, as well as *Sears List of Subject Headings,* a cataloging source discussed a bit later. Some publishers will suggest Dewey categories for their materials. Most book publishers cooperate with the Library of Congress to include CIP (Cataloging in Publication) data in their books. The CIP includes full catalog card information on the verso (back) of the title page of each book. Look at the CIP on the verso of the title page of this book as an example. Be sure to check the information against the source, however, since there are sometimes inaccuracies because the cataloging information is created before the final draft of the book. Of course, your own catalog has similar materials you can look up to see how they were classified by your predecessor.

The only trick in assigning Dewey numbers is that some centers have their own unique rules concerning specific collection areas. These include things such as the designation B or 921 for biographies that were discussed in chapter 7. Some rules can be more complicated, such as putting all career information under the Dewey number for vocational information, 371.42, rather than in the specific career field. A center may classify all career materials with this number even though information about becoming a doctor should, technically according to Dewey, go in 610.6 and information about being a historian should be in 907.2. These little "quirks" in a collection are developed by each center to assist its particular users, but you need to find out what they are before you get carried away with classification. They should have been written down somewhere in a cataloging guide. If not, look for all special collection areas or check similar material in the center's catalog before you classify it.

The Dewey number forms the top line of a call number (with the few exceptions noted in chapter 7). The bottom line is an indication of the author or, if there is no author (for some collective works and most AV material), an indication of the title. Obviously, *a, an,* and *the* are ignored when the first word in a title. Each center decides whether to use the first letter, the first 3 letters, or the entire author's last name or the title's first word. Going beyond a single letter speeds up the shelving process. Once you've assigned the Dewey number and author symbol to the call number, classification is complete.

For the sake of a few of you who may find a bottom line on a call number that is a combination of letters and numbers that bear no resemblance to the author's name, you've found the remnants of something called the Cutter system. Cutter was a librarian who established an elaborate code to designate authors' last names. School libraries used that code eons ago, but today it is used primarily by larger facilities, if at all. Some individuals are "newly" discovering Cutter. However, since the vast majority of libraries use just the author's last name, stick with that.

CATALOGING

Now we turn to cataloging, creating the bibliographic information for indexing the item. It is usually easier to deal first with the subject(s) headings for the item because this is the first access source for most users. It is important to list all subjects handled in depth within the item. There are standardized sources to help assign subject headings. One of these is the *Library of Congress Subject Headings,* which is used primarily by larger institutions— the ones who use LC classification. However, since LC is also used in MARC records (see the subsection later in this chapter), more libraries are using these headings, especially at the high school level. The entire LC subject guide is multivolumes and rather expensive. Subject headings suitable for younger students may be found in *Subject Headings for Children: A List of Subject Headings Used by the Library of Congress with Dewey Numbers.*

Sears List of Subject Headings

The most commonly used guide in schools, especially at levels below high school, is *Sears List of Subject Headings.* The purpose of *Sears* is to ensure consistency of subject headings assigned; it becomes an authority file of subject headings used in your center. Most catalogers place a checkmark in front of each heading when they first use it as a reminder for future use. Additional subject headings that the cataloger feels necessary to create are written in at the appropriate spot. If a cross reference is established from a subject, that is also indicated in the *Sears List.* See figure 10.1 as an example of such marking.

The subject heading chosen is usually for the item as a whole, not for individual chapters or parts. However, if the item covers several subjects in depth or if it includes a subject that is a major part of the curriculum or a special project, additional subject headings should be added. Many of the sources that suggest Dewey numbers also suggest subject headings.

Figure 10.1 Annotated Page from *Sears List of Subject Headings*

✓Birds (May subdiv. geog.)
    Names of birds are not included in this
      list but are to be added as needed,
      in the plural form, e.g. **Canaries**; etc.
    See also **Birds of prey**; **Cage birds**; and
      names of birds, e.g. **Canaries**; etc.
    x Bird; Bird watching; ✓Ornithology
    xx Animals; ✓Vertebrates; Zoology
Birds—Flight. *See* Flight
Birds—Habits and behavior
    xx Animals—Habits and behavior

handwritten annotation: ✓Ostriches;

handwritten annotation: ✓Birds - Gaspé Peninsula
    x ✓Gaspé Peninsula—Birds

·e engines. *See* Gas and oil engines

handwritten annotation: Gaspé Peninsula—Birds. See
    ✓Birds - Gaspé Peninsula

Gastronomy. *See* Cookery; Dinners and din-
    ing; Food; Menus

Ornamental plants. *See* **Plants, Ornamental**

✓Ornithology. *See* **Birds**

Orphans and orphans' homes
    See also **Child Welfare**
    x Charitable institutions; Dependent chil-
      dren; Foundlings; Homes (Institu-
      tions)
    xx Charities; Child welfare; Children—In-
      stitutional care; Institutional care;
      Public welfare

Osteopathy
    See also **Massage**
    xx Massage; Medicine; Medicine—Prac-
      tice

Ostrogoths. *See* Teutonic race

handwritten annotation: ✓Ostriches
    xx ✓Birds

Versification
    See also **Poetry**; **Rhyme**
    x English language—Versification; Meter;
      Prosody
✓ *xx* Authorship; Poetics; Rhythm
✓Vertebrates
    See also Amphibians; ✓Birds; Fishes;
      Mammals; Reptiles
    xx Zoology

A check (√) indicates that the heading has been used.

x indicates that a "see" card has
been made.

xx indicates that a "see also" card
has been made.

Sometimes a subject heading is needed, but the usual sources do not have an appropriate heading, usually because of timeliness—such as the Desert Storm operation. In these cases, the *Readers' Guide to Periodical Literature* or *Readers' Guide for Young People* (the latter is available only on CD-ROM) may be used.

A final consideration with subject headings is cross references. Sometimes a user needs to be referred to another subject for additional information, therefore a "See also" reference is needed. For example, Ostriches *See also* Birds. A user may look up a subject that is not listed in the authority guide, so the user is referred to the correct subject, as in Farming *See* Agriculture. As shown in figure 10.1, the see and see also references are also written into the *Sears List* as they are established by a cataloger.

Regardless of whether the index is a standard card catalog or an electronic version, there is certain common information users need. These include call number, author, title, place of publication, publisher, date of publication, physical description (number of pages or items), format, illustrations, subject(s), and, perhaps, a summary of the content. All these elements appear on catalog cards or in an electronic catalog. These elements are also part of MARC records.

MARC Format

MARC, *Ma*chine *R*eadable *C*ataloging, is a cataloging record that can be read and interpreted by a computer. Even if you do not have an automated system, understanding and using MARC format records prepares you for the inevitable time when your catalog will become automated. MARC format makes it easier for you to "talk" to other libraries about similar titles if you have computer access to the Internet or other database sources, even if your facility is not automated. Furthermore, if you buy precataloged materials from a reputable company, using the MARC format assures you that your cataloging is compatible with that of everyone else.

A MARC record divides bibliographic information into "fields" that are sort of like traffic controllers for a computer, signaling the computer to "go here for the author, go there for the publisher," etc. These fields are assigned "tags," three-digit numbers, much like Dewey numbers for subjects. The numbers use less space in the computer system, so instead of telling the computer the main entry, *an author with a personal name,* is Ann Wasman, the computer is told *100* is Ann Wasman. If the main entry is *an author that is a corporation,* such as American Library Association, the computer is told *110* is American Library Association.

Some MARC records in some computer systems are "fixed," meaning there are limits to what they can do. For example, they are limited to a certain number of characters in a field or to a certain number of fields in a record. The "fixes" are determined by the entity that is creating the records. Full MARC records are important in automated systems. Therefore, it's best to demand full MARC records.

To understand MARC just a bit better, following is an example of common bibliographic information with MARC tags and examples, in MARC tag order:

Information	*MARC Tag*	*Example*
Dewey number	082	027.8
Author—personal name	100	Ann Wasman
Title	245	New steps to service
Publication information:		
Publisher, place, date	260	American Library Association Chicago, 1998
Physical description	300	230 p. ill.
Summary	520	A guide for beginners in school library media work to assist them in the basic tasks required for their job

MARC records also have subfields that further delineate bibliographic information. The MARC format is more detailed than the example presented but perhaps the concept is now a bit clearer. MARC format is used to catalog all types of materials. If you are cataloging within an automated system, you need to know MARC. If you are creating cards for a card catalog and are using a computer program to generate them, you may need to know MARC. *Note:* An excellent source for a more-detailed description about MARC, specific brochures for various formats, and an excellent format guide to use for MARC cataloging are available from the Follett Software Company, address in appendix A. Another source is ALA's *Cataloging Correctly for Kids*, third edition, edited by Sharon Vuiderveld.

As mentioned previously there are varied ways to handle the cataloging of materials. If your facility has an automated system, you can use MARC format to create original records in the system for each item you purchase. Or, depending on the jobber or publisher, you can get a disc from them that has full MARC records for each item purchased. You then download it into your automation system, make necessary adjustments, and the items are ready for the shelves. You can also subscribe to a bibliographic database available on CD-ROM that has MARC records for titles published in the last several years. Using the ISBN, the LC number, or other bibliographic information, you can search the CD-ROM for a match to items you've purchased. You then download the information directly to your system or to a disk that is then downloaded into your automation system. (ISBN stands for International Standard Book Number, a unique number assigned to each title published in the world, although most third world countries' publishers don't use one. It is a means of identification that is used to obtain bibliographic information. For example, the previous edition of this title had as its ISBN 0-8389-0387-8. In the event you're curious, the first digit identifies the country of origin; the United Kingdom and the United States begin with either 0 or 1. The first group of digits, which can be up to seven figures long, is the publisher's number. The second group of digits identifies each specific book title and binding, so different bindings for the same book receive different numbers. The last digit is a check digit that verifies that this is an authentic ISBN.)

Anglo-American Cataloguing Rules

Another cataloging tool to know for proper cataloging, even though novices and most specialists in elementary and smaller facilities do not usually work with it, is *AACR2, Anglo-American Cataloguing Rules,* second edition. As its title indicates, this source contains the authorized descriptive rules for cataloging. It is used to determine correct access points for a main entry. It includes correct punctuation and format for main and added entries for all types of materials.

Creating Catalog Cards

If your LMC is not automated, you can create catalog cards by computer, or you can type your own from scratch. When creating catalog cards, you need a full "set." A set consists of

1. author card, usually the main entry, with the author's name on the top line
2. title card with the title on the top line
3. subject card(s) with the subject(s) on the top line
4. shelflist card, similar to the author card but with the ISBN, tracings, and ordering information—usually purchase-order number, price, source, and month and year of purchase (Tracings are used on the bottom of the main entry and shelflist cards to identify all additional cards made for each item. They are used when materials are withdrawn so that all catalog cards for each title can be traced and removed.)
5. cross-reference cards as needed
6. analytical cards (those that refer to parts of a work because of the significance of the pieces) as needed

Samples of homemade and vendor cards are shown in figures 10.2 and 10.3.

If you are creating your own cards, consider the following pointers:

When there is more than one author, place only the first one on the top line. Mention the others in the main body of the card after the title.

Figure 10.2 Homemade Catalog Cards

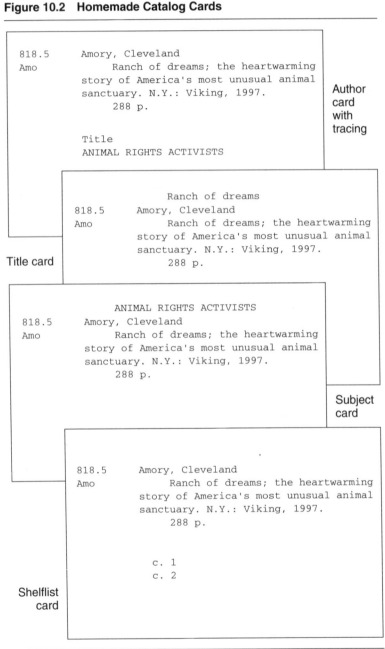

Figure 10.3   Vendor Catalog Cards

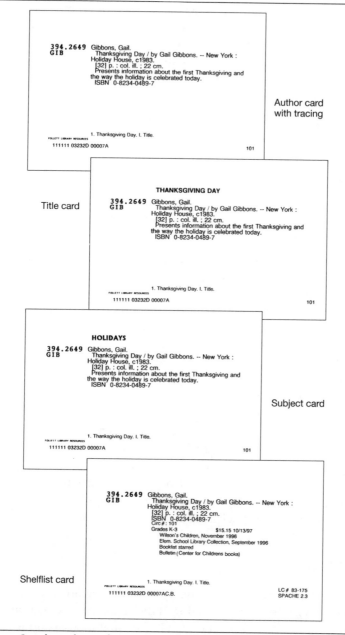

Source: Sample catalog card set courtesy of Follett Library Resources.

If there is no author, just begin with the title.

When a title is the same as the subject, or when a biography title is the same as the name of the person profiled, no subject card is needed *unless* you have a divided card catalog in which the author, title, and subject cards are in separate sections rather than in one continuous alphabetical order.

Capitalize only the first word in a title and those that are proper names.

Type subject headings in all capital letters.

If the title cannot be completed on one line, continue it on the next line at the second indentation.

Create a card for an illustrator only if she or he is significant.

If no publication date is given, use an approximate date enclosed in brackets.

There are three different indentations used on self-created cards. The first is for the call number, approximately 3 spaces in from the left edge of the card. The second is for the author, approximately 12 spaces from the edge. The third is for the title, approximately 15 spaces from the edge. The main entry, or author line, is usually the third line down from the top of the card. Added entries—title, subject, etc.—are placed on the line immediately above the author. Different catalogers, cataloging teachers, and cataloging guides may use different indentations. The important factor is consistency.

Self-created cards are a lot of work and trouble. The cards available from jobbers and publishers, as mentioned earlier, are worth their cost, especially if you have no clerical help.

FILING

With an automated cataloging system, entries are updated immediately. When a card catalog is the index to a collection, the individual cards need to be filed before that index is up to date and usable for patrons. Clerical staff or volunteers can be trained to handle this job, but they are usually taught to file "above the rod," meaning they do not drop the cards into each drawer but leave them on the top of the rod that holds the cards in the drawer. After you check their work for accuracy, the rod is pulled and the cards are in place.

Cards are filed by standardized rules: *ALA Rules for Filing Catalog Cards* second edition. The rules have changed over the years to coincide with the way computers deal with information. Your card catalog may have some hold-overs from the old days. If so, use an alternate title, *ALA Filing Rules,* which is more in line with other indexes and which considers formats besides books. The following list summarizes a few of the differences:

Old Way	*New Way*
Mc and *Mac* all filed as if they were *Mac*	Filed as they appear
Abbreviations filed as if they were spelled out	Filed as they appear
Numerals filed as if they were spelled out	Numerals from lowest to highest at the beginning of the index, before the letter *A*—symbols, then numerals, then letters
Same-word entries arranged in a hierarchy of person, then place, then thing	No distinction among persons, places, things, and titles—just by alphabet
Historical subdivisions in chronological order[1]	Historical subdivisions as written
Names compounded with prefixes treated as one word: Van Horn	Filed as they appear

---

1. Sears has changed the way historical subdivisions are handled so the dates now come first: *United States—History, 1861–1865—Civil War* instead of *U.S.— History—Civil War—1861–1865.*

Old Way	*New Way*
Words spelled two ways are treated as if there were one established way: color/colour	Filed as they appear

Most card catalogs interfile author, title, subject, cross-reference, and analytical cards in one large alphabet. A few split them up into separate author, title, and subject groups, each with its own alphabetical order. Some put author and title cards together but keep subject cards separate. It's an individual decision for each LMC. The shelflist card is always filed separately in an area accessible only to LMC staff.

Cards are filed alphabetically by the top line, word by word, and letter by letter within a word. Thus, *New York* comes before *Newton* because you look at each word. Some refer to this as the "nothing before something" rule, the way a computer would handle it. If the first word is *a, an,* or *the,* it is ignored and the second word is used. However, these articles are considered when they are *within* the title.

PROCESSING

The final task is processing. Again, for a fee many jobbers will provide materials totally processed and ready for the shelf, but it is worth the money to save the time. However, if you are determined to do it locally, processing will include the following steps:

1. Identify each item with the name of the school library media center, usually with a rubber stamp. The identification should include the address as well as the name so any lost items can be returned.

   Books are stamped on the inside of the front and back cover, the outside edges, the verso of the title page, and a page of your choice but always the same page—your "secret" page. The idea is that anyone who steals the book and removes the more obvious ownership stamps will miss the one that is on a page only you know. You may stamp in fewer places if that is the established procedure.

Periodicals and pamphlets are stamped on the cover and one other page—secret and consistent once again.

Audiovisual materials are stamped wherever you can find a spot but certainly on the container and as many of the components as possible. The rubber stamp may not work on AV materials, and you'll have to use pressure-sensitive labels. You can create these with a computer and printer, or you can purchase them.

2. The call number is placed on the spine of each book or container so it can be seen by users as they search the shelves. It is best to be as consistent as possible with this placement. Pressure-sensitive labels are useful for call numbers since they can be adapted to all types of media and come in a variety of sizes.

3. The call number, author's name, and title are placed on the borrower's card and the pocket that holds the card.

4. The pocket is placed inside the front or back cover of a book—whichever has been established by the LMC. For other types of materials it is placed wherever it fits.

5. If a date slip is used, it is pasted on the pocket or the page opposite the pocket, wherever it fits best. Some pockets have a date-due area included so no date slip is necessary. If you use a date-due card, it is inserted in the pocket when the item is checked out.

6. Mylar or plastic covers may be purchased to place over book jackets to keep them clean, protect them from wear, and make them more attractive.

7. Covers may also be purchased to place over current issues of magazines for protection. Some styles will also discourage theft.

When each item is ready to go to the shelves, it may be recorded on a form to keep track of additions and withdrawals. This step is up to each LMC. Figure 10.4 shows such a form, incorporating withdrawals as well. This form is an easy way to have a current tally of materials readily available for those who seek such information.

Figure 10.4   Record of Additions

BOOKS			
Date	Volumes added	Volumes withdrawn	Balance
7/98			4376
9/98	‖‖‖ ‖‖‖ ‖‖‖ ‖‖/ ‖‖‖ ‖‖‖ ‖‖‖ ‖‖‖ ‖‖‖ ‖‖‖ ‖‖‖ ‖‖‖ ‖‖‖ ‖‖‖ ‖‖‖ -75	‖‖‖ ‖‖‖ - 10	4441
10/98	‖‖‖ -5		4446
11/98		/// - 3	4443
1/99	‖‖‖ ‖‖‖ ‖‖‖ /// ‖‖‖ ‖‖‖ ‖‖‖ ‖‖‖ ‖‖‖ ‖‖‖ -48		4491
2/99	‖‖‖ ‖‖‖ ‖‖‖ - 15		4506

FILMSTRIPS			
Date	Item added	Items withdrawn	Balance
7/98			1245
9/98	‖‖‖ - 5		1250
10/98		/	1249
11/98	‖‖‖ /// - 8	// -2	1255
1/99	//// - 4		1259
2/99	‖‖‖ ‖‖‖ // - 12		1281

Classifying, cataloging, filing, and processing are all detailed tasks that require a great deal of time and effort from library media specialists who are already woefully short of time for all the tasks expected of them. Using the precataloged and pre-processed options available from jobbers and publishers saves time, and a specialist's time is worth far more than the extra money spent for this option. There is no way to put a price tag on the time the specialist will then have available to spend on jobs that more directly involve students and staff.

Part III

Dealing with
Details

11

Is turning it on all I have to do?

Equipment for and from the library media center

The library media center has long had to deal with equipment. In the "old days" it was a typewriter, then came audiovisual equipment and the copy machine. Today it involves a variety of equipment types used both in and outside the LMC. The common feature is that the library media specialist usually orders it, accounts for it, maintains it, and discards it when it's outlived its function. As a new library media specialist, your first item of business related to equipment is to find out exactly what equipment is your responsibility. In some schools such responsibility involves every item in the building, including computers and public address systems.

EQUIPMENT INVENTORY

When the extent of responsibility has been settled, it is time to find out what there is, where it is, and what condition it is in. The best place to start is with the inventory list. If there is no inventory list of all equipment, look for individual inventory cards or a database in the computer. If neither exists, check with the principal to see if some type of building inventory list includes equipment for which you are responsible. If there is no list of any type, you will have to create one.

The advantage of creating an equipment inventory list from scratch is that you get to set up the system your way. The disadvantage, obviously, is that the process will again eat up your precious time. First, you have to decide which format of the options available you're going to use for your list. Then, after reading the rest of the information in this chapter, you'll establish a record for each piece of equipment.

Now, you must physically locate all the audiovisual equipment and check it against whatever list you have (or create a list) for the following necessary information:

- manufacturer/brand name
- model number
- serial number
- inventory number
- accessories
- condition
- location
- purchase date, if available

It's also a good idea to indicate the type of bulb used, if it is a projector, and any other parts that may be needed and should be on hand. Some specialists prefer a listing system that includes space for notes about repair.

Then make a list of each piece that is on the record but not physically in the LMC or found in an alternate location. Obviously, this presupposes you're working from some type of list. When the missing-item list is complete, if there are LMC clerks or volunteers, ask them if they know where the items are. If that effort doesn't produce the missing equipment, take the list to the principal, or whoever you report to, and ask where these pieces might be. If the principal has no idea, ask permission to search classrooms and storage areas throughout the building. After all, if it can't be found, it can't be used or cleaned or repaired or listed for insurance. If you don't get administrative help, or if the search yields nothing, create a flyer or poster for the teachers' mailroom, lunchroom, and lounge. Make it somewhat light-hearted:

Missing: as listed below

Last seen at inventory during Stone Age

Answers to: Property of _____ School

Reward offered: cookies and lemonade

plus eternal gratitude to persons

with information leading to recapture.

No questions asked.

Contact Kelly Montgomery in the LMC

Then list all the missing items with appropriate details: type of equipment, brand name, model number, and serial number.

Perhaps within the first week of school individuals will come forward to indicate that they have the equipment or know where it is. Seize this opportunity to demonstrate good PR: no lectures, no recriminations, no intense questions. Find out if the informants need the equipment assigned to them for a long term or if they use it less than once a week and can share it with others by returning it to the LMC. Assure them that you will set up a schedule so they can have it whenever they need it. If the equipment is used frequently enough, or if the teacher is upset and possessive, indicate on your list who has it and drop the matter for the moment.

Checking Equipment

Once AV equipment has been located, check to see that it is clean and working. Sometimes a quick glance will be sufficient to see that it is in good repair, but a fast field test is best—and time-consuming. Remember, you will be expected to troubleshoot all equipment. Therefore, you may as well try it out before everyone else is back in school so that any mistakes of operation can be made in private.

This is also a good time to locate all the operation manuals for the equipment. Keep one copy for each model owned and organize the manuals in a file or three-ring binder, whichever format works best for you. Duplicate manuals can be given to teachers, or another file or binder could be set up for everyone's use. The remaining manuals can be discarded.

Labeling Equipment

If there are records indicating which teachers usually check equipment out for the year, set that equipment aside with the teacher's name on it. Then mark the circulation system indicating who is getting what, and put a memo in each teacher's mailbox letting teachers know their equipment is ready.

Once all—or most—of the equipment is found, it's time to decide exactly how to keep track of AV equipment. First, every piece of equipment should be visibly marked with the school name and an identification number. This number serves a purpose similar to that of a call number: It's a way to locate and track the equipment. It also makes it easier to inventory the items. The number can be etched on the machine with a special marker, but the simplest, most-visible way is to use black permanent marker or a small paintbrush and paint.

Indicate the type of equipment with an easy-to-understand abbreviation: TV, VCR, SL (slide projector), etc., and a number that is simply an accession number (TV-1, VCR-4). The inventory list should then reflect the number assigned. Possible abbreviations for equipment include:

Audio cassette recorder	CAS or REC
Audiovisual cart	Ct
Computer	COMP or PC or brand name: Mac, IBM
Filmstrip projector	FS
Filmstrip viewer	FV
Opaque projector	OP
Overhead projector	OV
16mm movie projector	MP
Slide projector	SL

Slide viewer	SV
Sound filmstrip projector	FSS
TV receiver	TV
Videocassette recorder	VCR

TRACKING EQUIPMENT

You'll need to establish a procedure for circulating the equipment. If the existing process seems to work well, use it. If not, there are other possibilities as outlined in the following sections.

Any of the following systems can be used by teachers on an honor system or by library media staff. The advantage of visible circulation systems is that teachers can easily use them on their own. In the case of a large scheduling board, they can see what's already out. The advantage of a booking system is that they can request equipment in advance.

Teachers sometimes, deliberately or unknowingly, take equipment without indicating they have it, creating major problems for the library media specialist who is responsible for the equipment. Some library media staff avoid this problem by personally checking out the equipment. Regardless of the system, the personal touch ensures far better control. But if the LMC staff is small and if the individual in charge of equipment is busy when a teacher stops by, the teaching staff becomes frustrated and difficulties can develop. What system works in each situation is dependent on the specialist, the teachers, and the climate of the building. Honor systems that work beautifully in one LMC may be disastrous in another.

Automated Circulation System

An automated circulation system can be adapted to include AV equipment. First, each piece of equipment must have a bar code attached in addition to the inventory number. Then you must create an inventory control record within the automated system and "attach" the bar code to that record. Establish check-out parameters, just as for materials. Finally, duplicate each teacher's borrower card or check out the equipment at the desk where the cards are located. Now check-out is a simple matter of scanning the bar codes on the equipment and the borrower's card.

Card-and-Pocket or Tag System

One method for keeping track of equipment uses a bulletin board with book pockets attached. Mark each pocket with either a teacher's name, grade level, or room number, depending on how you want to keep track. There is one pocket for every teacher, grade, or room. Attached to each piece of equipment is a card with its inventory number: CAS-1, VCR-2, TV-1, etc. If possible, glue a pocket to the equipment to hold the card or attach a punched card with twine or a garbage bag twist tie. When equipment is checked out, remove the card from the equipment and place it in the correct pocket on the bulletin board. Mark on the card the date circulated or the date due, whichever you prefer. When the equipment is returned, reattach the card. (See figure 11.1.)

Another method divides the bulletin board into two sections: In and Out. There are two sets of larger pockets (file folders can be cut to size and attached by tape) for each *type* of equipment (slide projectors, TVs, etc.). One set is on the In side, the other on the Out side of the bulletin board. Make cards for each piece of equipment with the appropriate code and inventory number (VCR-1) and put them in the equipment-type pocket on the In side. Teachers find the appropriate card, fill out the information you've determined (probably name and date taken), and put the card in the appropriate pocket on the Out side. (See figure 11.2.)

A third method uses a pegboard. Identify each peg or hook with either a teacher's name or a room number. Each piece of equipment has a tag on it with its unique ID number, probably hanging on an adhesive hook on the machine. The teacher simply removes the tag and places it on the peg with his or her name. (See figure 11.3.)

The fourth method uses long "reserve" book cards, one card for each equipment type. The cards are filed in a box where the teacher finds the card for the type of equipment needed and

Figure 11.1 AV Equipment Circulation Board

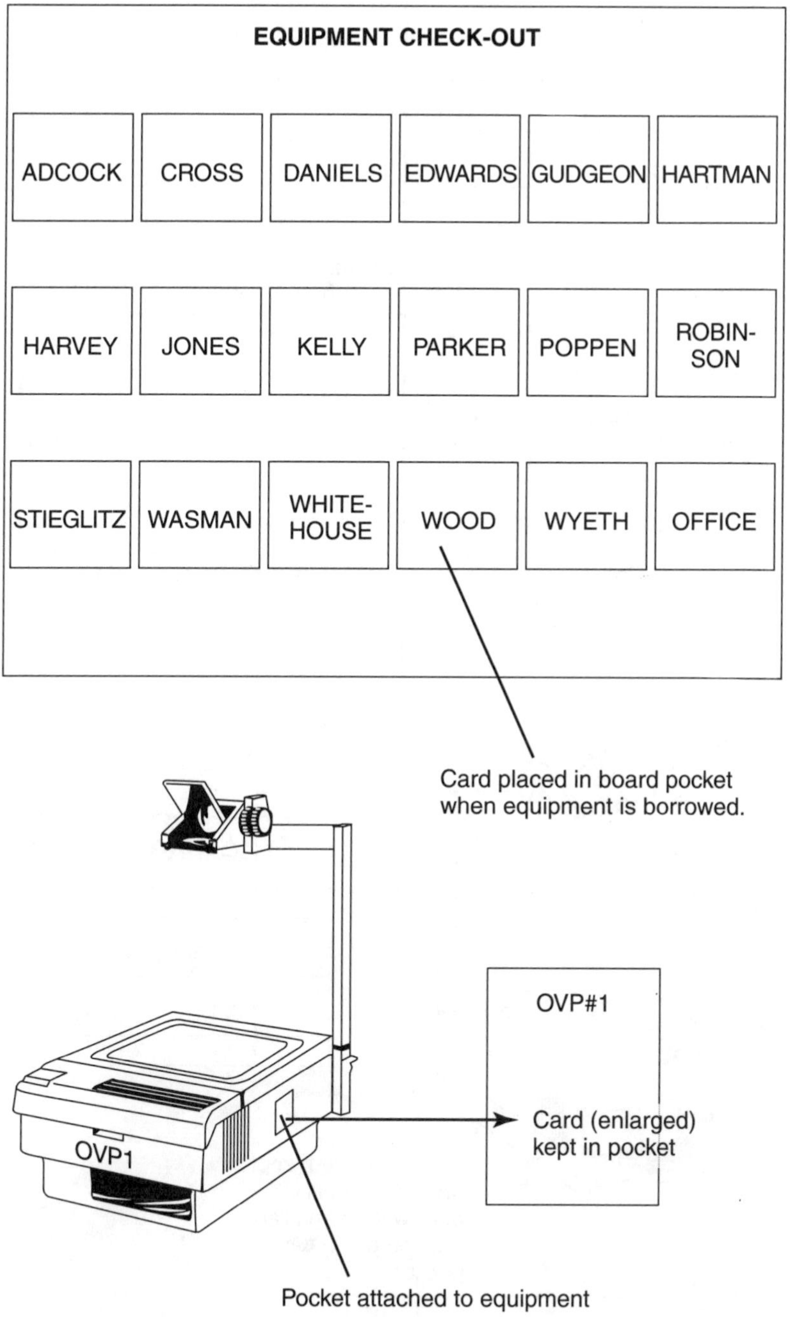

EQUIPMENT CHECK-OUT

ADCOCK	CROSS	DANIELS	EDWARDS	GUDGEON	HARTMAN
HARVEY	JONES	KELLY	PARKER	POPPEN	ROBIN-SON
STIEGLITZ	WASMAN	WHITE-HOUSE	WOOD	WYETH	OFFICE

Card placed in board pocket when equipment is borrowed.

OVP#1

Card (enlarged) kept in pocket

OVP1

Pocket attached to equipment

Figure 11.2 In/Out AV Equipment Circulation Board

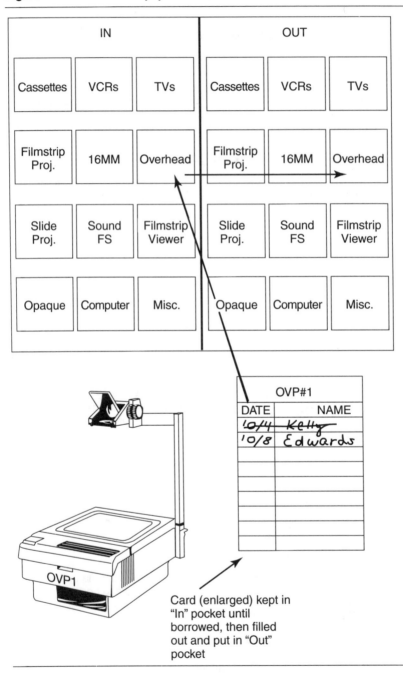

Card (enlarged) kept in "In" pocket until borrowed, then filled out and put in "Out" pocket

Figure 11.3 AV Equipment Circulation Pegboard

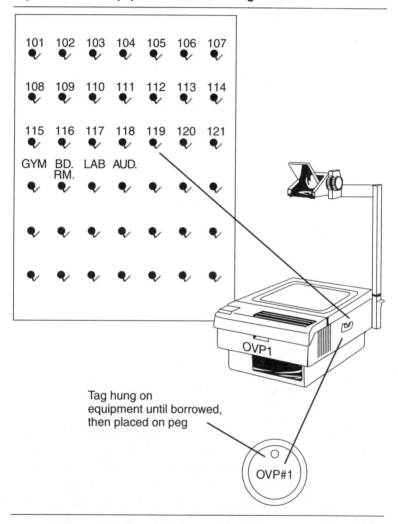

Tag hung on
equipment until borrowed,
then placed on peg

writes the inventory number, his or her name, and the date, and
refiles the card in the box. If it's more convenient, you could use
a pocket for each card on a bulletin board. (See figure 11.4.)

Paper and Calendar Systems

One circulation system uses a special circulation sheet created
for each piece of equipment. The paper may be lined or not,

Figure 11.4   AV Equipment Circulation Card

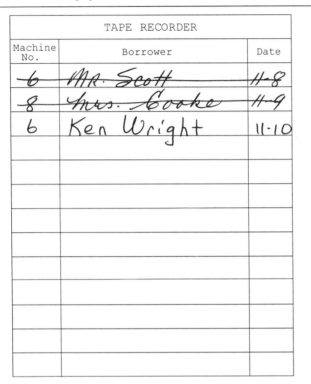

	TAPE RECORDER	
Machine No.	Borrower	Date
~~6~~	~~MR. Scott~~	~~11-8~~
~~8~~	~~Mrs. Cooke~~	~~11-9~~
6	Ken Wright	11·10

laminated or not. The top portion includes the equipment type, make, model number, serial number, and unique ID number. Below that are columns for date borrowed, teacher's name, date returned, and notes. Keep the sheets in an easily accessible place, preferably a three-ring binder. Teachers find the sheet for the equipment they're taking and fill in the information. When they return the item, they again find the sheet and cross out their names. If the sheet is laminated, use a special marker so the entry can simply be erased when the item is returned. (See figure 11.5.)

A calendar system may use any type of calendar, so long as it has plenty of space under each date, or it may use a teacher lesson-plan book. Equipment is booked under the appropriate date and time with the equipment ID number and the teacher's name. For example, Monday may show "8–9—Jones, VCR-2/

Figure 11.5 AV Equipment Circulation Sheet

CAS #2

Type: Cassette Recorder   Make: Panasonic   Model: 360   Serial No.: 4628972B

Date borrowed	Teacher	Date returned	Notes
10/4	Edwards	10/6	bulb blew
10/7	Daniels	10/7	
10/11	Robinson		

TV-1." When equipment is returned, the entry is crossed out. Obviously, a weekly or daily calendar works best in this method. (See figure 11.6.)

A scheduling board is another type of calendar that can be used to track equipment. The board may be a large chalkboard or a huge laminated board. Across the top write Monday through Friday, plus Next Week. Down the side are time periods appropriate to the situation—class hours or hours of the day. Equipment that is taken is booked in the appropriate spot with the teacher's name and equipment ID number. When equipment is returned, the entry is erased. If equipment is needed for the next week, the teacher marks that column with his or her name, day, hour, and the equipment needed. At week's end, check the board for outstanding equipment, which is entered under Monday, and add requests for the next week. (See figure 11.7.)

Request sheets can be used most effectively when equipment can be delivered. Distribute copies of the request form to teachers (and keep some in the lounge, department offices, and the AV equipment area). Teachers indicate what they want and

Figure 11.6 AV Equipment Circulation Calendar

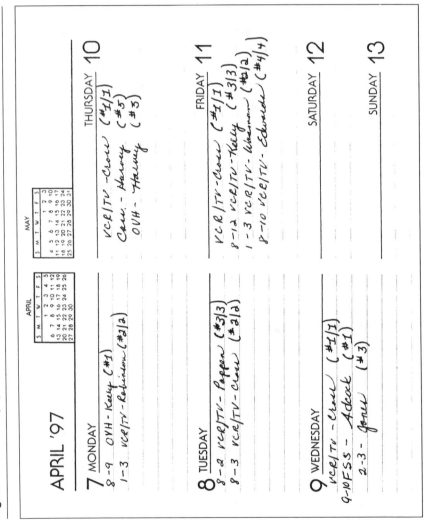

Figure 11.7 AV Equipment Circulation Scheduling Board

Time	Monday	Tuesday	Wednesday	Thursday	Friday	Next Week
Before						Kelly-OVH Wed. all day
8–9	Pessina-OV3 all day	Kelly-OVH#1 Hartman-MP#3			Brown-VCR5, TV5 Edwards-VCR2, TV2	Wasman-Cas, OVH-Tues
9–10			Evans-FSS 3			Jones-VCR, TV-Fri
10–11	Cross-VCR#2/ TV#2				White-VCR 1, TV1	
11–12	Harvey-Cas #3 all week					
12–1				George-FSS4	Poppen-VCR4, TV4 Adcock-VCR3, TV3	Daniels-VCR,TV-T-Th 12-3
1–2						
2–3						
After	Bd. meet-OV		PTA-VCR, TV		Band boosters-Cas	

133

when by filling out the form and returning it to you. You then transfer the information to whatever checkout system is being used and see that the equipment is delivered to the teacher at the appropriate time and picked up when the teacher is done. Student AV assistants are critical to the success of a delivery/pick-up system, but it may be worth the effort to find and train them because teachers appreciate this help. (See figure 11.8.)

DECIDING WHAT IS NEEDED

AV equipment falls into two categories: equipment used in the LMC and equipment circulated to other areas. Usually library media specialists are most comfortable selecting what is going to be used in the LMC because they are more familiar with how it will be used. However, the same principles, considerations, and research in selecting equipment for the LMC should be applied to the selection of circulating equipment. The research may involve sitting down and discussing the equipment with the staff members who will be using it or having them look through equipment catalogs to show you what they want.

Figure 11.8   AV Equipment Request Form

REQUEST FOR AUDIOVISUAL EQUIPMENT

TEACHER _____ ROOM _____

Needed:

_____16mm projector	_____Microphone
_____Screen	_____Cassette player
_____Slide projector	_____Opaque projector
_____Filmstrip projector	_____Overhead projector
_____VCR	_____Extension cord
_____TV	_____Other:

DATE NEEDED _____ HOURS _____

Projectionist Required: YES _____   NO _____

Equipment in the Library Media Center

Equipment within the center also seems to fall into two categories: staff use and patron use. Interviews with library media specialists have yielded a "must have" list for their own use: telephone, computer, copy machine, fax machine, and VCR/TV. In addition, computers specifically for library use can vary greatly in terms of added peripherals. The most obvious add-on is a printer, but other specialists indicated they needed a CD-ROM drive and a modem. Some respondents simply said they needed "the Internet." One comment heard repeatedly was that the computer is the replacement for the typewriter, a replacement that allows better administration. Word processing improves communication and databases facilitate inventories and purchases; the computer stores tremendous amounts of both in far less space and with quicker, easier, better access than do other systems.

Equipment within the center deemed necessary for patron use includes a copy machine, computers, printers, CD-ROM equipment, Internet access, microform readers, book trucks, AV carts, and an automated system. Some LMCs have AV equipment set up on a permanent basis for patron use, from TV/VCR setups to filmstrip viewers, cassette players, slide viewers, and Internet access. Some LMCs also function as the computer lab for the building. What is in the LMC is an individual decision depending on the program and services of each center as it activates its role within the educational program.

One item that has caused endless frustration to many library media specialists is printers for computers. When an LMC has computer stations with CD-ROM databases or electronic catalogs, students often are allowed to print out what they need, with resulting paper jams. Buying a quality printer that will feed easily with minimal jams is important for your sanity.

Other kinds of equipment the center may use are AV or computer production equipment—from 35 mm and video cameras, transparency makers, tape recorders, and laminators to scanners, digital cameras, and digital editing equipment. Such equipment allows teacher-inspired materials to be custom designed and locally created on site. These materials are frequently more helpful than commercial materials in teaching because they are specific to teacher and student needs. In addition local production equipment may be used to record student activities for public relations or evaluation of student products.

Production equipment raises yet another concern for the library media specialist. Who is to use this equipment? If the specialist is expected to produce the requested items, there is yet another time crunch. If teachers are expected to do it, there may be problems in their learning to use the equipment effectively and carefully. If student aides are recruited to create locally produced materials, they will need to have a training program on production processes so they can use the equipment effectively and efficiently. All these problems can be solved with planning and consideration of all the issues involved.

Selection Considerations

The primary selection criterion for any equipment, regardless of where it's located, is use—how it will be used and by whom. For example, if teachers want a VCR simply to play videocassettes, there is no need to select a VCR that will record up to seven different programs in a period of two weeks. However, a programmable VCR might be of primary importance if you are asked to record programs off the air for teachers. On the other hand, some teachers are adamant about having a remote control for the VCR so they can control it from different areas of the room, but that feature often drives up the price and is available only on models with more features.

Which brings up another criterion in selection: cost. Home-use, or consumer, equipment that can be purchased at nearly any local electronics store or discount house is cheaper than equipment created for commercial use. It's cheaper because it isn't made as well and can't last as long, especially when exposed to different users, some of whom may be a bit careless. Some specialists avoid the multiple-user problem by assigning less-expensive equipment, such as cassette recorders, to the same individual. Some of these same specialists point out that equipment changes so quickly they don't want to invest the additional money in a more-durable piece of equipment that will outlive its use.

Others feel it's better to spend more money up front on equipment that will last for a longer time, recognizing that such equipment will inevitably need repair. The difficulty with repair is that it's hard to find repair shops locally that will work on this equipment. The repair services from AV jobbers, although usually reliable, often take a lot of time and are expensive. Such repair issues also must be factored into a decision because their cost drives up the price of equipment even more. With less-expensive equipment, the repair factor is handled by simply replacing the equipment, which some feel is less expensive in the long run than continued repairs.

Another consideration in selection is compatibility. Consistent purchase of the same types and models of equipment makes it easier for teachers to use the equipment. They learn how to operate a particular model and don't have to deal with learning how to operate other models. While this may seem insignificant, it is frustrating to staff members to get, for example, a different model tape recorder every time they request one. The controls are located in different spots and may be of different types—a toggle switch on one, a punch button on another, and a dial on a third. It's these little things that can cost a teacher time and patience.

Therefore, it is a good idea to ask teachers how they like particular models of equipment or what piece of equipment they prefer. Involve them in evaluating what works well for them. Ask them about operation. Teachers are more interested in something that is consistent and reliable than in state-of-the-art or low-end budget models. Once you find equipment that satisfies the needs of the users, keep ordering it.

The order procedure is covered in detail in chapter 14, but one aspect to mention here is that of writing specifications. Part of the ordering process for equipment is to create specifications for the equipment, a task often undertaken by the business manager, who has no idea what you need and why. Usually specifications include details about how the equipment is constructed, wattage, etc. To get the same equipment as that you currently have, specify the brand name and model number. Then use the company's catalog to copy the specifications itemized in its literature.

Regardless of the type of equipment, who is using it, or where it is located, if the administration determines the library media center is responsible for equipment, it is your duty to take care of it. Taking care includes ordering, cleaning, inventorying, training, and doing whatever is necessary to make the equipment available to and usable for those who need it for the educational process.

12

Where do I put everything?
Facilities

Library media centers are organized with the same major factor in mind as everything else that happens in, around, and about the center: use. In evaluating what areas are needed, where they are located, and how much space should be allotted, the underlying questions must always be How is it used? How does its use relate to the program and the rest of the center?

DEALING WITH CLUTTER

The most common problem new library media specialists have with a facility when they begin a job is clutter, frequently accompanied by dust. They are nearly overwhelmed by the sheer amount of "stuff" everywhere, making easy movement about the center and easy access to its materials nearly impossible. Furniture is too close together; shelves are so loaded they begin to bow. Sometimes all the material doesn't fit on the shelf, so it's piled on top of the other material. File cabinets are hard to close because of all the papers in them; equipment is on the floor, jammed together on one cart, or stuffed in a closet.

Some specialists experience claustrophobia; others fear they'll never find what they need when they need it. All are perplexed: On the one hand they're told "don't throw anything out the first year," on the other they know they can't function with the disarray they've inherited. So what to do?

First, talk to your administrator. Make the problem yours; don't blame your predecessor. Tell the principal you cannot learn the collection as quickly as you need to because there is so much material that there doesn't seem to be time or space to organize all of it. Explain that you need to reorganize it into a system that will work better for you. Mention that your predecessor kept a lot of material from long ago that obviously worked with curriculum units; however, you want to concentrate on the units for this year with the current curriculum and evaluate the other items later. Ask for some storage area elsewhere in the building that you can use for a year, but still have access to, so that if you store something for later evaluation that is suddenly needed, you can get to it within a reasonable time.

If there is clerical or volunteer help, ask them what things they remember being used the most; ask teachers what items they need the quickest, easiest access to. Find out if anyone is willing to take seldom-used material on long-term loan until it can be dealt with. "Loan" some of the extra furniture to classrooms, asking teachers to use it until you can prepare a proper home.

Start with the least-used areas of the collection, according to past circulation records. Take the items that have been used the least—those with check-out dates ten or more years ago—and place them in order in labeled boxes that can go into storage elsewhere. If there's no magazine index, get rid of back issues of magazines more than a year old unless they are used for research. In that event hold only five years' worth.

Ask volunteers to help sort and categorize materials from the file cabinet into boxes. Test equipment; any that doesn't work should be shuffled off to the garage or boiler room or any "hole" until there is time to determine the problem and the cost—or even possibility—of repair. Look carefully at the shelves. Is it possible some of the piled up stuff could be taken care of by shifting the collection? Because such shifting is a major and messy undertaking, some people just pile up materials rather than move them. If that's the problem, move the collection to accommodate the extra materials.

Remember, this is where you have to live eight hours or more per day. Approach it the way you would moving in with a spouse or roommate who stores mounds of junk. You need to reach a compromise so you can have your space until you can slowly work your way into other areas.

SIGNAGE

Another thing new specialists realize is that a library media center frequently is lacking proper signage to guide users to collection and service areas. Signs that are colorful, clear, and large enough to be readable from a distance are a necessary part of any facility. If signs are lacking, or if they are faded, hard to read, or ugly, replace them.

Signs for major areas should be visible from the entrance and main traffic path. They should be two sided so they may be viewed from either end of the LMC. Although color is important, it should not be disruptive. For example, some specialists are tempted to use eye-catching hot colors, but these are often very hard to read, especially if there is bright light.

Coordinate the signs in style, size, font, and color so they appear to be well-planned and complement the facility and each other. They should be durable, easy to clean, and easy to update. Nice-looking, inexpensive signs can be computer-generated, then laminated for endurance. Signs should guide users to collection areas and services. They should also relay concise, effective directions. Each center needs a large, well-marked map near the entrance, especially if collection areas have been moved.

ELECTRICAL CONSIDERATIONS

A third problem area is lack of electrical outlets and proper voltage. Before you can possibly consider automation, you must solve any electrical problem. Check the outlets in your facility—Where are they? How many are there? How accessible are they in the current arrangement? If they don't seem adequate, talk to the maintenance person in your building, explain the problem, and ask for suggestions.

AREAS AND FUNCTIONS

The major areas—and their typical functions—in an ideal center include

Circulation	Located near the entrance/exit of the center to facilitate easy check-out and check-in, this area includes space for returning items, housing materials to be reshelved, storing check-out records, and transacting patron business, along with signs and displays and, possibly, a copy machine.
Browsing area	Located near the periodicals and other areas where readers may want to indulge in casual reading, this area should have casual furniture and adequate space to display new materials to entice readers.
Reference area	If possible, located somewhere near the circulation desk or another area where staff assistance will be close by, this area obviously needs shelving for the reference collection and table space to work with reference material. The catalog and other indexes should be located near this area.
Class area	This area provides space for large-group instruction, a sort of "home base" for LMC activities while classes pursue their information

	needs, with tables for working with materials.
Small-group area	In this space students can work together on a group project; it may be as small as one table.
Main reading area	Here are found tables for using materials from all collection areas where individuals, small groups, and large groups can work independently or together.
Listening/viewing area	This is an area away from the "quiet" parts of the center where users can use AV materials. It may have individual carrels with electrical outlets for equipment to save space and cut down on noise.
Stack area	Shelving for the major part of the collection is in this area. Most LMC shelving is around the parameters of the center, which frequently limits the creation of some of the special areas mentioned.
Periodicals storage	Current issues of periodicals are housed near the browsing area; back issues are in a separate area as need dictates. This is preferably a controlled-access area.
Equipment storage	The area should preferably be located near a door so equipment can be moved in and out with minimum disturbance.
Office area	It's important to have a space where the library media specialist can work in private, keep personal files, and find a moment's peace.
Work area	This busy area is where receiving materials, cataloging, processing,

mending, and all the necessary activities of the center can be spread out, performed, and left when need be.

Other areas
In an ideal facility, there is also a media production area, a teacher area, a computer lab, a display area for new materials and student work, and for elementary levels, a storytelling area.

Ideally, the center would easily accommodate all these functions with plenty of space, suitable furniture, and appropriate shelving. However, in the practical world library media centers are often active and crowded. The possibility of space in quantity, specifically designed for the library media program, is more of a dream than a reality. Library facilities, properly equipped, are expensive. Few schools have the funding to provide attractive and durable furniture, adjustable shelving of the right height, carpeting, and all the amenities to create an environment that is welcoming while being a haven, conducive to quiet while accepting the noise of students busy at work.

Fortunately, library media people have a marvelous talent for creating usable, attractive spaces out of whatever they have to work with. Additional good fortune comes as teachers and students rely on the facility and as administrators and parents see its value. Then ways can be—and are—found to make the facility more usable and comfortable. The following sections provide some tips for creating your optimum LMC.

Creating Space

Many library media specialists use shelving units to create specific areas in the facility. In so doing, they give consideration to which portion of the collection is placed where so that use is not compromised. For example, a browsing area may be set off by the magazine, fiction, and short story collection shelves. There may be a reference area that is separated from the rest of the space by counter-height shelving for reference materials. (Such shelving has the added advantage of being an appropriate height on which to place reference books while using them.)

Another aspect to consider in creating these distinctive areas is discipline. Students love to find spots where they can't be seen. Shelving units, especially tall ones, sometimes accommodate this desire with drastic results, such as vandalism. Being able to see into as many areas as possible is a key to monitoring student behavior and avoiding discipline problems. It is one reason library media specialists who use stack areas for nonfiction, for example, move the ends of the shelf sections against the wall so students can't go behind the shelves to hide out. It is another reason that library media specialists use counter-height shelving, even though taller shelves would accommodate more materials.

Shelving should be as adjustable and attractive as possible. Shelves need to be geared for the age group they serve. The younger the students, the lower the shelves. Shelves must also be sturdy enough to hold heavy reference books. The width of shelving aisles is dictated by policies on serving those with disabilities.

A final aspect unique to facility design is security. Locating material that has a high loss potential near the circulation desk or staff areas may discourage thieves. Paying attention to shelving placement can prevent not only discipline problems but vandalism. However, if such logical steps do not reduce loss and damage, a security system is the answer. A security system should be placed near the exits, although the unit will eat up space—another factor to consider for placement.

Redoing and Revamping

As with planning anything else, renovating the appearance of the center, whether it's a complete remodeling job or merely rearranging shelving and furniture, needs to be carefully thought out. Once again, reading and visiting can give you some great ideas. So can browsing through library supply catalogs that may have some unique storage units that can solve a special problem.

Rearranging the LMC requires input from those who will be using it. Ask faculty members for their opinion unless it's something relatively minor or something that won't have an impact upon them, such as rearranging the workroom or your office. The more involved the rearranging or remodeling, the more their ideas should be solicited. Involving staff members can lead to some really good suggestions, a sense of ownership by being part of what is happening, and a lessening of the impact of complaints from those who get upset if something is changed without their knowledge by using the old technique of strength in numbers. (If you change it, someone may complain loudly, even going to the principal. However, if other faculty members have given input about the change, it's a lot harder to have a complaint taken seriously.)

Another good idea is to involve students, if they are old enough, and a representative from the maintenance staff. Not only might these audiences generate some good ideas, they may bring a perspective no one else has ever considered.

One of the best ways to involve faculty is not only through discussion. They can help by evaluating proposed floor plans, reading about center design and use, and visiting other facilities. Let them hear experts from other facilities, especially newly remodeled LMCs, talk about things to consider when planning a center for the future. The more information all of you have about what is possible, what is practical, what is essential, and what is in the world of tomorrow, the more likely you will be an effective team.

13

Is there a simpler way?
Automation

It has surely been apparent that I am a proponent of automated systems. These systems can simplify library media tasks, especially the clerical ones, and expand the potential and possibilities of research. They can offer the library media staff advances in record keeping, storage, and information retrieval. Even though computer-based systems for typical tasks such as circulation, inventory, acquisitions, serials control, and cataloging have been around since the 1960s, they have not become affordable to school library media centers until the recent decade.

THE BEGINNINGS

The first systems were large and expensive, used by large academic and public libraries that could afford them. These electronic beasts required constant and expert assistance, so staff was added simply to keep them going. Through the following years the systems became faster, more efficient, capable of more storage, and smaller—just as everything else in the computer world has.

Turnkey systems, prepackaged systems that included hardware and software, were sold as units. Some companies developed software designed to operate on the specific types of computers that libraries owned. Separate staff was not needed for these options, which made their prices more reasonable. Many of these systems were developed by computer experts without library experience or input. Although the units could store information about items, they were not geared to the specific needs and uses of the library field. Furthermore, the cost was still prohibitive for many schools.

The microcomputer further increased the speed, storage, and efficiency of systems while decreasing the size and cost. Schools that once couldn't seriously consider automation now saw it was possible. Experienced vendors who specifically targeted the library media field not only used library media personnel to advise them but hired people from the field to assist in designing, implementing, troubleshooting, and improving their systems. Vendors also increased the options available so they could provide packages to all types and sizes of libraries. These vendors can be found at national and state meetings, and their advertising is carried by nearly all professional magazines. Anyone looking for a system should seek vendors from these sources.

CONSIDERING A SYSTEM

When considering an automated system, there are a variety of factors to address. The one that first springs to mind for most people is cost, which must be considered in all aspects, not just the price of hardware and software. There are also ongoing costs to maintain the system, staff time to deal with it, expenses to convert from the traditional method to automation and ongoing system upgrading. Many system vendors will offer packages that incorporate such costs.

The primary consideration, of course, is what you want the system to do. Do you want the entry in the electronic catalog to look like a catalog card or to use a menu approach? Do you want an inventory component that may be done at any time, without having all items checked back in? Is the system easy to use for you, for staff, and for students?

Automation can be set up for one or several functions, but a fully integrated system is the best way to go. If you're going to all the trouble to input records for circulation and inventory, you already have the basis for a public access catalog, which will greatly improve service to patrons. Some vendors have integrated systems that can be purchased in modules to spread out the cost so that you can purchase your circulation system, then cataloging, then public access, and so on. Some can arrange payment programs to avoid a large one-time expense.

Besides purchasing an integrated system, also select one that uses full MARC records. Others may be less expensive, but your system will not be able to "talk" to other systems, and should you need to upgrade or improve later, you may well run into difficulties. Full MARC records will be invaluable to you in undertaking retrospective conversion, the process of changing existing records into an automated format. You will be able to download records from databases if your system is full-MARC compatible, and it will be much easier when purchasing precataloged materials to dump them into your automated system.

Retrospective conversion (converting existing records into automated ones) is, in itself, an involved task.

Does a vendor offer the service?

In what format?

At what price?

With what degree of "hits" (matches)?

If the vendor's program doesn't get a hit, will the vendor convert from the shelflist—or return the shelflist to you for conversion?

How easy is it for you to add or modify records in the system?

What type of back-up is available?

In what format?

Other technical aspects to think about include the type of bar codes used. Can the scanner read different label types? If so, you'll be able to buy materials from jobbers who can supply the bar codes. You may also be able to buy bar codes from library suppliers instead of the automation vendors. (It's cheaper and sometimes faster that way.) How many tasks can the system perform at one time? How many users can it accommodate? If the system locks up when four borrowers hit the same record, it may lack the type of flexibility you need. Can other systems be networked into this one? For example, can CD-ROM databases be added? Are the manuals easy to understand for setting up, using, and troubleshooting of the system? Does the vendor offer on-site training programs? Is prompt, quality support service readily available?

Also inquire how easy—and costly—it is to upgrade the system. Once it is functional, it will be a tremendous boon to your services, but technology marches on with constant improvements. Your students and staff deserve those benefits too. It's entirely possible that a vendor will build this factor into the price.

When choosing a system, research as much as possible. Contact several vendors; carefully read their literature, and visit sites that have their systems in operation. Ask questions, and ask for demonstrations. Talk to other library media specialists, and read professional journals and books. Attending professional organization conferences will be especially valuable because they often have programs, exhibits, and even discussion groups about automation.

As you discover information and learn about automation and what it can and can't do, share the information with faculty, students, and administration. Let them know their concerns and questions are important. If they ask a question or raise an issue you don't know about, tell them you'll find out, then do it. Consulting staff members is wise, not because they'll have knowledge of such systems, but for that feeling of ownership that comes with involvement. Besides, they may have some considerations you haven't thought about.

14

How do I manage the money?

Budget and acquisition

Before beginning a discussion of funding—how it is determined, spent, and accounted for—it's important to agree on a few terms. The budget process is normally the procedure for requesting funds for the program. The acquisition process is how you order, receive, and mark items as your own. The accounting process is the procedure to verify items and amounts for payment, keep track of what's been spent, and authorize payment. All of these processes, however, usually get lumped together as "budgeting," which can become pretty confusing for a newcomer.

The majority of money allotted and spent on a library media program comes from the local school budget. Usually each building is given a sum, and the principal of a building is responsible for the allotments to all departments within that building. In some districts, a district library media coordinator is responsible for the budgets in each center. The system used to determine and account for the funds of the library media center varies from state to state and district to district. However, most states now have established a statewide accounting system for state reporting so that there is consistency in account numbers representing specific types of purchases.

The budget, or fiscal, year in school systems encompasses the school year: July 1 of the current year through June 30 of the next. Most purchase orders are expected to be obligated by March or April 1 (depending on the school system), items received, and payment issued by mid-June so that everything is cleared away before the end of the fiscal year. Anything billed so it does not clear the system by June 30 is charged to the next year's budget.

The business office in the district verifies receipts, processes the paperwork, and presents the checks to the school board for authorization—a process that may take a minimum of one month. Thus, most school library media specialists do the majority of their ordering in the fall, although they obviously evaluate and build their "want" files all year. Exceptions may include periodicals, equipment, and supplies that may be ordered at the end of one school year with instructions to "bill after July 1" so the items are charged to the next year's budget.

BUDGETING SYSTEMS

Through the years a number of budgeting systems have been used within schools. These include the programming-planning-, zero-based, and line-item budgeting systems. Each is described in the following sections. Whatever budgeting system is used, the budget requests for the next school year are usually due early in the calendar year. While this may seem too far in advance to have a good grasp for the next year's needs, it is essential so that the business office can proceed through the involved process of approval, posting, hearings, etc., that are required for a school district to adopt a budget for the upcoming year.

Programming-Planning-Budgeting System

The programming-planning-budgeting system, or PPBS, incorporates justification for each budget item requested in terms of how it advances a companion plan for development. This plan, created for a three- to five-year period depending on the district, is first developed by the appropriate staff members. Each budget item requested relates to the first year in the current plan. As each new year comes up, the entire plan is reevaluated and an additional year is added on the end. Thus, the long-term plan is in a constant state of evaluation and revision.

In its most formal style there are categories in PPBS budget request forms that usually show the item requested, quantity, unit cost, and total cost and its justification and relation to the long-term plan. A budget request sheet, which is only for the current year, might look as shown in figure 14.1.

Zero-Based Budgeting System

The zero-based budgeting (ZBB) system begins with the premise that everyone's budget is zero. The budget is then built from the bottom up according to what is needed most. Request forms include details of an item's purchase and an explanation

Figure 14.1 Programming-Planning-Budgeting System Request Form

Account	No.	Item	Cost	Relation to plan
252.44-3	200	Fiction books	$1,500	Implements year 1 of plan to replace fiction books at a rate of 5 percent of collection each year.
252.44-5	10	Video tapes	200	Applies to year 1 of plan to build video collection in curricular areas designated by science teachers
243.22	1	VCR	400	Equipment is not in plan; unexpected theft of VCR this year necessitates purchase
243.22	1	Security system	7,500	Originally in year 2, previous savings and longer life of AV equipment allow this purchase to be made within total anticipated budgetary requests
TOTAL			$9,600	

of importance. Budget requests then proceed to the next most-important budget item, etc., so that the last item listed is the last thing needed (in other words, the first to be cut.) In ZBB the on-going items needed just to keep the program functioning typically get mentioned first, and program expanding, developing, and growth items are mentioned last. A possible budget request sheet from ZBB is shown in figure 14.2.

Figure 14.2   Zero-Based Budgeting System Request Form

Account	No.	Item	Cost	Rationale
252.44-1		Office supplies	$200	To keep the LMC operating, we need pens, pencils, envelopes, stationery, paper clips, and general office supplies for record keeping and administrative use
243.20		Equipment repair	500	To supply equipment for classes and individuals, we need to maintain existing equipment in good repair
252.44-3	300	Books	2,250	To replace the 100 titles past records have shown will be lost, damaged, or disinte-grated due to age during the year and to add 200 titles in all areas of the collection to maintain currency with the new curriculum adopted in science and social studies
252.44-5	10	Video tapes	200	To add video tapes to support the newly adopted consumer education curriculum
243.22	1	Overhead projector	350	To replace unrepairable overhead used by math department
243.22	3	Audio cassette recorders	250	To increase the equipment available for intensified literature appreciation curriculum
TOTAL			$3,750	

Line-Item Budgeting System

The line-item budgeting system is typically used most in schools. In this system the requester lists line-by-line the item needed, the amount requested, the category number assigned, and, perhaps, an explanation of the item's relation to the program. Some districts include the amounts previously allotted for the category and a rationale for any increase. Some library media specialists add these figures so the administrators can see their past allotments. (See figure 14.3.) Line-item budgets typically restrict expenditures to exactly what is approved. Thus, a shortage in one area cannot be covered by an overage in another.

Line-item budgeting systems often do not incorporate a justification for or an explanation of the items requested. That may pose a problem for school library media centers because their requests require a background understanding that most administrators, especially business officials, do not have. Thus, it is wise to attach a separate document that includes a detailed explanation of the requests and their relation to the program.

Defining "Supplies"

In some districts there are only two types of expenditures for departments or grade levels: supplies and capital outlay. In these districts *supplies* means any materials to be used for the educational program that are temporal, in other words, those that won't last long. They will be used up, or consumed, by student use and time. Therefore, supplies, in this view, include not only office supplies but also periodicals, books, AV materials, and everything else except equipment and furniture. Thus, if the line item is "supplies" and particular types of materials are listed below that heading as subcategories, funds can be transferred back and forth between the individual subheads because none are given a specific amount or listed as a separate line item. The same is true of the capital outlay line. In this case the sample budget will appear thus:

Supplies $4,250   books, AV materials, computer software, periodicals, office, and processing supplies

So if the specialist plans to spend $750 on periodicals and doesn't, the remainder could be transferred to the computer software to make up an overage in this area.

Figure 14.3   Line-Item Budgeting System Request Form

Account	Line Item	Last Year	Current Year	Next Year	Reason for Increase
254.101	Books	$2,000	$2,500	$3,000	To keep the collection up to date and to enlarge it in the fields of drugs and ecology
254.102	Periodicals, newspapers	400	450	500	Increased costs and adding magazines for the new humanities course
254.103	Nonprint materials	2,400	2,950	3,500	To add laser discs and computer software in the field of science
254.104	Binding	100	150	175	To keep the collection in good, attractive condition
254.105	Supplies	250	300	300	No increase anticipated
254.106	Furniture	0	0	500	To add 1 study carrel for independent study
254.107	Equipment	75	250	500	TV/VCR combo for individual student viewing
254.108	Processing	150	200	200	Processing kits for materials
254.109	Film/video rental	300	350	350	No increase anticipated
254.110	Equipment repair	175	175	200	Increased labor costs
254.111	Memberships	25	25	50	State dues have increased
254.112	Conferences	100	100	100	Board of Education policy
TOTAL		$6,035	$7,285	$9,440	

SAMPLE BUDGET PROCESS

The following is a quick "walk through" of a possible budgeting scenario. The specialist is told budget requests are due by *x* date and must be presented according to whatever system the district is using. The specialist develops requests. Clearly it is too early to list every title of every item that will be needed, and few, if any, school districts require that information at this time. However, they do want a general idea of what types of items will be purchased. The specialist's requests may look like the one shown in figure 14.4 (with an added column for the particular account number used in the district for that type of item).

In some districts the total request—all items—may go on a single budget form. In others, capital outlay items may be placed on a separate form.

Capital Outlay

The capital outlay category, regardless of budget system or process, is considered part of the building; it's more permanent than supplies. Capital outlay items require maintenance and repair and are not "consumed" by the educational program. (Obviously, these budget experts have not seen how some teachers and students use the equipment.) Because the capital outlay category is a big portion of every budget, including items such as copy machines, furniture, football seating, security systems, etc., a district may require that each capital outlay request be itemized. In other words, AV equipment—$5,000—must be broken into types of equipment, numbers, and amounts.

Capital Outlay: AV Equipment

5 audio cassette tape recorders @ $50	$ 250
3 VCRs @ $400	1,250
3 TVs @ $400	1,250
5 overhead projectors @ $275	1,375
1 computer @ $875	875
TOTAL	$5,000

Figure 14.4   Sample Preliminary Budget Request

Item	Amount requested	Explanation/Justification
Supplies	$ 250	Office and related supplies for processing, repairing, and circulating materials and equipment
Books	2,500	Reference and regular circulating books as requested by students and staff and as identified for curricular projects, includes funds to update 5 percent of the science collection
Audiovisual materials	500	Materials requiring use of equipment that relates to classroom projects and teacher requests as well as development of visual and audio materials for use within the LMC
Computer software	250	Software programs for the computers within the LMC
Periodicals	750	Periodicals, pamphlets, and necessary indexes for current information
SUBTOTAL	$4,250	
Repair	500	Maintenance and repair of AV and LMC equipment
Capital Outlay: AV equipment	5,000	Cassette tape recorders, videocassette recorders, TVs, and overhead projectors to replace equipment that is no longer reliable
GRAND TOTAL	$9,750	

Using a line-item budget system, money requested for the tape recorders and not spent in total because the costs were cheaper could not be shifted to cover the extra cost of the computer. How the money is allocated and whether it can be shifted depend on what system the district sets up and how it enforces accounting. Therefore, check out your district's requirements carefully.

Bids and Specifications

Another aspect of budgeting is the bid and specification process. Most states have a procedure whereby items that total more than a certain amount and are bought from a single supplier must be bid by specification. The purpose is to get the best price. The limit may be, let's say, $5,000. So if all AV equipment is purchased from one source, those items must go through the bidding process. To bid, each supplier of that type of item who wants to be considered for the order gets an opportunity to give an estimate. The district provides them with a list of items and specifications.

If the specifications are very general—five audio cassette tape recorders—the supplier can bid any product that fits that description, any make or model. If, however, the specification is more specific:

> 5 Sharp tape recorders, model 334 with pause
> control, autostop, push-button operation, tape
> counter, and headphone jack

that is the *only* cassette recorder a supplier can bid and legally expect to get the order.

However, if the district business manager adds the words "or equivalent" to the specifications for each item, it is again open to the supplier's discretion to include anything that appears to be equal. Then the district must determine that it is an equivalent. Technically, the supplier that meets the specifications with the lowest price *must* be granted the order.

Some school districts will get around the low-bid requirement by including general specifications, such as "all equipment must be delivered, with operator's manuals, by 30 days within receipt of purchase order." It may add a general specification that the company must also provide repair service. Some districts will send separate orders for lesser amounts to suppliers, thus getting around the funding requirement. Realistically, however, bidding—if specifications are done correctly so you don't get stuck with junk that fits a general description—is an excellent way to get quality items for the best prices. It is also why school library media specialists must watch the cost of their bulk orders to jobbers.

Justifying Requests

Let's return to the budget request process. Following whatever format the district requires, all the requests are totaled from throughout the building, and a final tally is sent to the district office. Because budgets are nearly always over the amount the district can afford, a process begins to cull the budget items until the total is a reasonable amount that will fit the district's needs. Typically, the building principal makes the determination for the building, and that's why a good relationship with the building principal will help the library media center's budget. Principals who understand the purpose and the needs of the LMC will be more supportive (and generous) than those who don't. Sometimes principals will meet with all, or some, individuals to discuss whether their budget requests can be reduced. Sometimes they'll return the forms with a request to cut an amount or a percentage; sometimes, the worst option, they'll just decide on their own and cut the one thing that was really needed.

It's a good idea to have a separate budget justification document regardless of the budgeting system. Such justification may include background on the requested items. For example, the book allotment request may be accompanied by a summary of the number and age of items in each collection area with an indication of what must be expended to bring the collection areas up to date. The justification may also include a statistical summary of circulation as well as the numbers of classes that used specific collection areas for projects. Perhaps the budget justification itemizes equipment requests and indicates the condition of each type of machine including the number of machines that are no longer operable, number that are questionable and likely to break down during the year, and again, usage of each machine.

A budget justification document is an excellent opportunity to use the standards discussed in chapter 2. Reference to the standards can demonstrate what a quality program should have and why. The budget justification should be professional in appearance, brief in content, and succinct in presentation. Using charts and tables is an excellent idea because this document becomes your advocate, your rationale, your educational tool for the budget reviewers.

Yet another factor to recognize when preparing a budget is how administrators react to certain terms. For example, using *technology* as a term to incorporate computer hardware and software, as well as laser discs and players, seems to impress them. Most administrators want their buildings to be current in thinking and to demonstrate an attempt to incorporate technology into the education of their students. It follows that the items marked "technology" will then receive approval with minimum objection.

Repair is also an area that is not questioned unless the amount is outlandish. Administrators often seem more willing to spend money on keeping what they've got going than on buying more-reliable replacements. One trick sometimes placed into a budget request is an outlandish figure for repair, reflecting what would be needed to bring outdated equipment up to the reliability standards of new equipment. This budget also included an alternative—at a lesser price—to buy new equipment to replace the old, demonstrating that one new reliable item could replace three older pieces that needed frequent repair.

Sometimes the budget system used in a district totally cuts out the library media specialist's input. The principal sets a figure, tells the specialist what it is, and asks for a proposed expenditure breakdown. Such a procedure certainly cuts down on the time a specialist must spend preparing a request, but it often also curtails the amount that can be purchased. In this circumstance the only alternative left to the specialist is an aggressive, consistent campaign—accompanied by plenty of documentation —to educate the principal about the needs, services, and role of the library media center. Enlisting teachers, parents, and students to advocate the library media program is also a big help.

MISCELLANEOUS FUNDING SOURCES

Other sources for LMC money include local, state, and federal grants; gift funds from groups or individuals; fines; and fundraising. The procedure to request such funding is dependent on the district and the funding source. Fines, gifts, and fund-raising dollars are usually handled through an "activity" account set up in the building for groups such as athletic boosters, cheerleaders, clubs, etc. Procedures for requesting and spending the money may vary from school to school. If no clear method of record keeping is set up, establish one yourself for all funds at your discretion so there is never a question about where the funds went. Keep receipts and invoices so there is proof the $10 check written from the account to you was reimbursement for items you bought for the LMC. Faulty record keeping of discretionary funds can be grounds for dismissal if a question is raised and there is no proof.

Gift money from PTA/PTOs or businesses should also follow strict accounting practices. Soliciting such funding becomes a PR job unless it's an established practice that the group donates a specific amount each year to the LMC. Most fund-raising money is from book fairs sponsored by the LMC. These are a good source of money, especially before Christmas, but they require a lot of work, usually mean closing the center, and demand exacting records. Book fair record keeping goes beyond keeping track of funds the LMC may receive to include an exact inventory of what items arrived, which were sold, and which were returned.

ACQUISITION

Once a budget is established, the next step is to acquire the requested items. Some school districts are so overwhelmed by the variety and quantity of materials the LMC needs that they limit orders to only two or three per year, forcing the specialist to order all books, for example, from a jobber who can handle a large order. It is easy to understand the business office's position: If purchase orders are sent for only a few items at a time, hundreds of purchase orders may be generated, each taking time and money to process through the system. The problem is compounded if school library media specialists must first fill out a requisition for the items, then receive permission, then proceed with the purchase order. However, limiting ordering in such a fashion undermines your opportunities to purchase materials as needed and creates cataloging and processing backlogs that could be eliminated if purchases were spread out.

Purchase Orders

In most districts, the actual purchase order (P.O.) is created by staff in a business office at either the building or district level. In some places, however, the library media staff is permitted to create the purchase order. Under this condition, the specialist is not usually required to have a requisition form first; the purchase order, in effect, is the requisition.

Some districts dictate that every item ordered (for example, every title) must appear on the purchase order followed by individual cost and total cost, which differs only if there is more than one copy of a title ordered. An easier task for the library media specialist, however, is to indicate a general description of the items with their total numbers and prices on the purchase order and attach order slips or sheets of paper with individual titles specified. The difficulty with this method is that the purchase order is not set up to accommodate it. A sample of a completed purchase order of this type is shown in figure 14.5. Note that the order number (which applies to each item) and the cost (which is the individual item cost) are then left blank.

In some districts the library media specialists can take advantage of phone, fax, or online ordering offered by publishers

Figure 14.5   Sample Purchase Order

Ship to: ABC School Library Media Center 1515 Happy Way Lane Anywhere, IL 60000		Bill to: District 000, Attn: Accounts Payable 1900 Business Road Anywhere, IL 60000			
Account No.	*No.*	*Item*	*Order No.*	*Cost*	*Total Cost*
252.44-3	100	Books per attached slips Includes preprocessing and catalog cards Also note attached supplemental list DO NOT EXCEED total shown			$750

and jobbers. They follow up by creating a standard district purchase order form indicating the order is a confirmation of a phone (fax, or whatever) order on whatever date the transaction took place. Other districts do not permit this latitude because there is a concern that the budget may get out of control and that budget areas may be overspent if the district's procedures to maintain control over budget areas are not followed. It is essential to talk with your predecessor or someone familiar with the budgeting and ordering process to find out exactly how your district is set up and what is expected of you.

Jobbers and Publishers

Whether to use a jobber or a publisher for ordering materials is usually an individual decision. Jobbers give discounts, but so do some publishers. Jobbers often supply precataloged or preprocessed materials, but so do some publishers. Jobbers can offer books from a variety of publishers. Publishers can nearly always supply any of their titles that were ordered, while jobbers may back order items and delay shipments. Publishers sometimes have trouble filling orders in late fall when their inventory is lowest. Remainder houses, which specialize in purchasing publisher overruns, frequently have their best supplies in late fall. Jobbers' supplies are about the same year round.

Whichever source you use, be sure to add to the total order any extra costs for options as well as to subtract any discounts. When using a jobber, if you're concerned about spending all your budget within the budgetary time limits, include a main order and a supplemental order. The supplemental order consists of titles to "fill in" for any items the jobber cannot immediately supply from the main order. If you use this process, you also need to place a "do not exceed" notification with a specific amount to remind the jobber of your budget limit. Otherwise, the jobber may ship and bill everything from the main *and* supplemental lists. In addition, indicate to the jobber or publisher how long back ordering is allowed. For example if you want the order canceled after 60 days of waiting for a back order, indicate "no back orders after 60 days." Obviously, the time of year may determine how long to hold open a back order. The closer you are to the end of the fiscal year, the less time you'll wait. You may reach the point of declaring "no back orders."

Knowing What Is Ordered

When ordering books, AV materials, computer software, and other general material items, it is essential to keep track of what is ordered and its status. Many automation systems have a built-in method to incorporate items on order. If no such feature is available, you have to develop a method. Check to see what your predecessor did, and if it works well, use it. If it's not workable for you, develop one.

Many specialists use a database program on their computers to generate lists of materials that are then attached to a purchase order. They can then check this database to see if they've already ordered a title or to file notes on its status, deleting the item when it is finally shelf-ready. Others use order cards or multicopy order forms they purchase from a library supplier. (See, for example, figure 14.6.) Whatever technique you use, the same information is needed for all orders and for all tracking systems: author, title, place of publication, publisher, date, edition, ISBN, price, source (jobber or publisher), purchase order number, and status.

Figure 14.6   Order Card Form

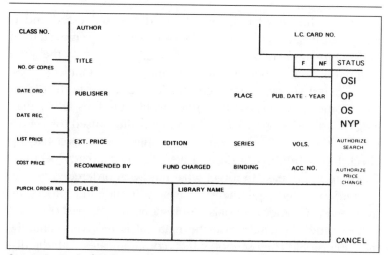

Source: Courtesy of Highsmith, Inc., 1997. Further reproduction without written permission is strictly prohibited.

Those who use multicopy order forms then create files within their shelflist of the items on order. The top copy of the form is sent with the order. Another copy is attached to the district office copy of the purchase order. A third is filed alphabetically under author (or title if there's no author) and another copy is filed under the purchase order number. Any additional copies may be sent to teachers to inform them an item is ordered, or the extra copies may be kept and used when the items arrive. After the material is received and checked in, the copy filed under the purchase order number is removed, placed with the item, and used to track it through cataloging and processing. The copy in alphabetical order may be moved to a new file marked "arrived," or the copy form may be marked with a code indicating that the material has arrived and is being processed. Any other copies may be sent to teachers to let them know the material is in.

Some specialists use the various copies of the order form to track the item through its different stages, initially filing all the copies under the author, for example, then tearing off and filing other copies elsewhere as the items come in. So a slip may be filed under "on order," then "received" or "back ordered," then "cataloging," then "processing" so the specialist can track it. If this seems to be more complicated than necessary, use what works for you.

When the item has been cataloged and processed and is ready for the shelf, all copies of the order form are removed from the system and may be sent to staff members to notify them the material is on the shelves. The advantage of the multicopy system is that it allows you to keep track of an order both by purchase order number and by author in flexible files rather than lengthy lists. The purchase order number file is used for checking the items in, and the alphabetical file is used as a backup check to confirm that a desired item has not already been ordered. It is very easy to forget what has been ordered.

Ordering AV equipment is usually a different procedure from ordering other materials. Equipment may be part of a joint district order, in which case the material is received centrally, then shipped to each school, which communicates with the district office to be sure all equipment ordered is received.

ORDERING SPECIAL ITEMS

Books and audiovisual materials follow fairly standard ordering procedures. Periodicals, equipment, and supplies sometimes have other factors that must be considered.

Periodicals

Periodicals are usually ordered from a jobber whose service makes ordering easier than sending individual purchase orders to each publisher. Some jobbers offer discounts or provide specialized services, such as a missing-copy bank for missed issues. Typically, you order from the periodical jobber once a year. While most schools do this in the spring for periodical subscription terms to coincide with the start of school, others will order in the fall for periodicals to start in January. It all depends on what works for you, but obviously, if you do not subscribe to titles over the summer, it's best to have fall start dates.

Most periodical jobbers will send a list for renewals, which you then update by adding titles or deleting them. Sometimes jobbers will send separate lists if you order or delete a title at a time other than the normal cycle. In such cases, contact the jobber to make arrangements for one total list each year at ordering time.

Most periodical jobbers will provide forms to use to indicate problems: titles that didn't come, duplicates, or expiration dates that don't match the jobber's records. To assist the jobber, keep up to date on receiving and recording titles. Requesting an issue in January that didn't arrive in October makes it impossible to receive that issue. Frequently, the magazine publisher will then assign credit; the subscription period gets lengthened, and problems emerge in rectifying magazine expiration dates with your and the jobber's records. Many library suppliers have cards available to track magazines as they arrive. (For example, see figure 14.7.)

Supplies

Supplies are ordered from library suppliers or local office supply retailers. Office supply items may be purchased cheaper locally, and they certainly arrive sooner. However, some specialty items

Figure 14.7   Periodical Check-in Cards

Monthly Magazines

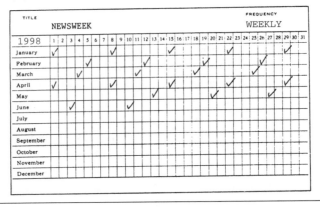

Weekly Magazines
Daily Newspapers

for libraries must be ordered from a library supplier. It's a good idea to comparison shop in the different catalogs until you get a sense of who supplies the type of item in the format you want at a reasonable cost.

The types of supplies you purchase depend on your own situation. For example, you may generate your own forms for periodical check-in, etc., rather than purchase them premade from a jobber. Whatever you decide, you will need

general office supplies—folders, labels, paper clips, staples, pens, pencils, notebooks, and three-ring binders, paper for copiers and printers, etc.

circulation supplies—date-due slips or cards, borrower cards (if nonautomated), pockets, date-due stamper, reserve cards, overdue notices, circulation-record cards, and periodical files

cataloging and processing supplies—ownership stamp, labels, book jacket covers, magazine covers, catalog cards (if nonautomated), mending tape, and transparent tape

audiovisual supplies—-cords, bulbs, cleaners, batteries, transparencies, marking pens, and laminating film

student supplies—first aid kit, needle and thread, erasers, rulers, and compasses

automation supplies—bar codes, date-due cards or slips, and diskettes

ACCOUNTING

When you place orders, create your own record in your bookkeeping system to keep track of what is spent and what is remaining in each account. This record may be in paper format (see figure 14.8) or on a computer database. At the time of ordering, the amount entered is an estimate; there is no way of knowing price changes or discontinued titles, etc. When the order arrives and is verified, an invoice should be included (or follow shortly) that shows the exact price. You must then update the ongoing account control record to show the actual amount and the actual balance. Use a separate control sheet for each account code.

Figure 14.8   Sample Budget Account Record

ACCOUNT NUMBER: 254.101					Budgeted Amount: $10,000	
Date Ordered	Pur. Order	Vendor or Source	Est. Cost	Invoice Date	Actual Cost	Balance
10-1	2754	Baker & Taylor	575.00	10-25	510.75	9489.25
10-5	2756	Bound-to-Stay-Bound	125.00	10-30	125.00	9364.25
11-1	2803	National Geographic	25.50	11-20	25.50	9338.75
11-1	2804	Supt. of Documents	20.65	11-25	20.65	9318.10
11-15	2822	N.C.T.E.	18.75			
11-15	2823	Wilson	42.00			
11-15	2824	A.L.A.	34.75			

The district office usually sends a monthly accounting sheet for each account for the LMC. Check it carefully, remembering it reflects actual expenditures and may, or may not, include obligated funds. Check over the figures recorded for each purchase order, and be sure they match your own. Watch out for purchase orders you don't recognize, and call for an explanation if any appear. This is one way to discover if teachers are being allowed to purchase books and AV materials for their classrooms rather than going through the LMC. Keep your records and your copies of purchase orders for three to five years. On occasion you'll need to use a purchase order to track information about an item you received. Similarly, items ordered one year may show up the next year.

Receiving Items

Whatever system is used to order equipment and other items for the LMC, there must also be a standardized procedure for receiving it. When an order arrives, it should not be opened until a copy of the purchase order and a list of what is to be included for that purchase order is on hand. First, each item should be examined to be sure it's in acceptable condition before marking the purchase order that the item is received. Flip through the pages of books to see if pages are upside down, stuck together at the top, backward, or missing. Open AV materials to see that all components that are part of the item are in fact there, and test the equipment.

When items are acceptable, mark the purchase order with a check for each item received, and pull the order forms from the purchase order file. Then send the list to whoever handles accounts payable at the building or district office. Sometimes the invoice is sent from the district office to the library media specialist for authorization. Once again, each district has its own system, and you need to find out what it is.

The company will usually send a packing list that itemizes everything sent on the order. Check this list against the purchase order, note any discrepancy, and forward the information to the business office. The packing list will also indicate items that are on back order, discontinued, out of stock, etc. Note such information and mark your records accordingly.

As items are received, stamp them with the library media center's ownership stamp and attach any security devices. Then place them on shelves designated for new materials. Set aside unacceptable items to be returned for credit.

Budgeting may be one of the most confusing aspects of your job. Not properly tending to it can cost you money, and loss of funds translates into loss of materials. If you have problems effectively requesting materials and justifying your requests or keeping track of what is spent and what is obligated, ask for help. Your principal or any other individual in the building who also has to request and account for funds would probably be willing to help you get off to the right start. If it's still a problem for you, find a volunteer who would be willing to help you keep track.

Part IV

Working with People

15

Will I always be alone?

Assistants, volunteers, and clerks

Perhaps you are one of the lucky ones with clerical assistants of some sort. If so, be grateful and keep them by treating them well. If the administration threatens to delete their positions, fight like a wild cat to keep them. It has surely become painfully clear that the mere acquiring, evaluating, controlling, circulating, maintaining, and recording functions of your job are rather overwhelming—even if essential. Having help to fulfill these tasks releases you to work with students and teachers. However, if you're like many beginners, you're out there alone, and you need help. Where do you turn?

USING STUDENT ASSISTANTS

Look first at a readily available source: students. Student assistants—properly trained, consistently praised and appraised, and encouraged to recognize their vital role within the program—can be a boon. They can save you time, energy, and effort and give you the added bonus of getting to know members of the student body individually.

Any student assistant program must be carefully planned and prepared. It must be a vital component of the program rather than a haphazard, by-chance endeavor. From recruitment of students to assessment of their abilities to development of their roles to evaluation and reward of their efforts—all aspects need to be thought through. Once you develop a plan for student assistants, present it to the principal for administrative support. After administrative approval is given, share the proposal with teachers to sell them on the value of assistants to the LMC program and to the students. Also convey the plan to parents so that all individuals who are part of a student's world are aware of what is being proposed and why. Only then should students be encouraged to sign up for an assistant's position.

It has often been said that things are worth what they cost; if you get something for nothing, it's worth nothing. If students perceive assistant positions as free labor, they will value their participation accordingly. Students need to see that being an assistant is a position of worth, an opportunity to learn, a contribution to the school, and a recognition of their ability and desire to share their time and talent for the well-being of their fellow students and their teachers. Consequently, all students who volunteer should be given an opportunity to participate.

Just Like the Real World

Viewing assistants as employees elevates the job, simplifies the process, and offers students an experience they can use in other situations. Student assistants should receive their own

- job description
- list of job tasks
- proposed work schedule
- job application
- recommendation form
- interview
- LMC tour
- training schedule

- job handbook outlining expectations and procedures
- time card
- job evaluation form

Obviously, the forms and procedures need to be adapted for the appropriate age groups. By using this structure you will get an idea of what the students are interested in, what their abilities are, what teachers and parents feel are their strengths and shortcomings, and how well they perform.

Point out to students that this experience is preparation for the time they enter the work world outside school. They should know that you can be a job reference for them when that time comes. They should understand that the entire procedure—notification of acceptance, training, work schedule, and regular evaluations—is the same as what they would encounter in any job. They should be treated as any employee—from official notification of acceptance to the moment of bonus or dismissal.

Job Applications

The job application should be structured like a real one, adapted to the age group. (See figure 15.1.) Younger children may be asked to take the application home and fill it out with their parents.

Regardless of the student's age, the parents' signatures should be required so you know parents are informed and supportive. The time limits—one hour per day, or whatever schedule you've decided—should also be in information sent home so students and parents know what time commitments are involved.

Encourage students to obtain recommendations from parents, teachers, neighbors, coaches, club leaders, religious leaders, etc.—people who know them. Request that students return a set number of recommendations with their application forms. (Use a form similar to that shown in figure 15.2.) If necessary, the recommendations may be sent separately by the recommenders but with the understanding the student may see them.

Figure 15.1 Sample Student Assistant Application Form

Name: _____ Grade: _____ Teacher: _____

Address: _____ City/Zip: _____ Phone: _____

1. Previous work experience—list any work, including volunteer, church, or clubs, etc.:

2. What types of work do you like to do?

3. Is there any type of task that you would prefer not to do?

4. Activities—list any clubs, organizations, hobbies

5. Why do you want to work in the Library Media Center?

6. What days and hours would you be available to work?

7. Please include at least two recommendations from people who know you. (Use the attached forms.)

I have read this application and approve of my child's participation if chosen as a student assistant.

_____   ☐ I would like to be present for any
(Parent's signature)   interview. A convenient day/time
                                         for me would be

_____

The application should include a section where parents can indicate if they wish to be present when the student is interviewed and, if so, an indication of a convenient time.

Interviews

Interviews must be conducted in private, not in the busy, noisy world of the LMC. If it's too busy during the school day, set interview times for before or after school. Keep the interview brief and to the point. Ask questions such as:

- Why would you like to volunteer in the LMC?
- What are the things you like to do best?
- What day and time would be most convenient for you to work?

Figure 15.2 Sample Student Assistant Recommendation Form

Recommendation for ___(student name)_____

Made by: _____ Address: _____ Phone:_____

The student named above has indicated a desire to join the Student Assistants staff at the ABC Library Media Center. To help us better know this student, please indicate your knowledge of this student and his or her abilities, talents, and work habits.

How long have you known the applicant? _____ In what capacity? _____
What do you consider his or her outstanding characteristics?

How would you rate this individual on

	Good	Fair	Poor
reliability	☐	☐	☐
consistency	☐	☐	☐
responsibility	☐	☐	☐
willingness to work	☐	☐	☐

Comments:

Please add any information you feel would be helpful in evaluating this individual's application:

Signature: _____ Date: _____

Return this form to the student or mail it to Annie Anybody, ABC Library Media Center, 554 Pleasant Way, Anywhere, IL 60000. (Please note that we may share this information with the student.)

- What do you like best about the LMC?
- Is there anything you would like to ask me?

Add any other questions that seem pertinent to your situation or this particular student.

Begin the interview with an explanation of the function and importance of the assistant, an overview of the types of tasks, an indication of how notification of acceptance is given and training is set up, and a description of the evaluation process. Conclude with a set time when the student will be notified of acceptance or not, an opportunity for the student to get clarification of any information not understood, and a handshake and thank you for the student's time.

Training

Conduct training with no more than five students at a time. A larger group removes the personal touch that is needed to get the program off to the right start. Each student should have a training manual. First, acquaint them with routine job procedures: what to do if they'll be absent, how to fill out and file their time cards, what they are expected to wear, how to behave, and how to handle questions or problems. Then they learn the general tasks they are all expected to do and the specific tasks assigned to each one.

Each assistant should receive a copy of the work schedule, which should also be posted in the office or workroom in an area that's for "staff." In creating the work schedule be watchful of students who will work less effectively if paired together because of social interaction. As a conference presenter at AASL in 1997 stated, "I've found that one student aide per period is a whole aide. Two aides is half an aide, and three aides is no aide at all." However, if work areas are scattered far apart and youngsters know they are expected to work in their assigned area, the problem may not emerge.

When developing a schedule, you obviously need to consider the way the school day is structured, and you need to gain cooperation from teachers. The time allotments will be taken from students' study time or recess or other times when teachers will release them. Accept that students will not have time available every day but more likely once or twice per week. The before and after school schedule should also allow students days off. Any task, no matter how carefully it's presented, can become boring if it must be repeated too frequently.

You may want to create task lists for students so that they can keep track if they're expected to perform several jobs. To create a task list, ask yourself: "Do I need to do this or could an assistant do it?" The answer will obviously be affected by the ages of the students involved. For example, junior high and high school students may be adept at checking materials in and out; younger students may not. While all ages may sort and shelve books, younger students may have problems with magazine dates.

During an assistant's first three or four days, be nearby so they can ask questions until they feel comfortable. After they are ready to be on their own, periodically check on their progress. Also develop a system for regular evaluation, perhaps every two or three months, and let the students know the schedule.

Incentives

Reward, recognition, and advancement are important to demonstrate that student assistants are, in fact, valuable. Consider a special treat occasionally, a small gift at holiday time, a birthday card, certificates, or special privileges such as answering the phone or learning to use the Internet in private sessions. Maybe you'll design a regular program of incentives, such as:

1 month of work	coupon for the school book store
2 months	letter of commendation sent to teachers and parents
National Library Week	breakfast in the LMC before school
monthly or each semester	special lunch with the principal for the outstanding assistant

You might generate public recognition of all assistants through an article in the school paper or local paper about the program and the assistants' value. Think about the types of little things that make you feel good and adapt them for your assistants. Watch for incentives in other fields—restaurants, motels, industry, and business—and adapt them for the library assistants.

An overlooked recognition for student assistants is advancement. As adults we like promotion, we like feeling we've advanced from one stage to the next; children are no different. Perhaps the assistants could be organized into teams, and team members could advance to team leaders as they gain experience. Perhaps the teams could have consultants who gain these positions based on experience and effort. Consultants could be in charge of displays or bulletin boards, train other assistants, act as troubleshooters for computers, or assist other students in the center. These special duties would be performed on an occasional basis.

Being an assistant should also be an opportunity to learn. Let assistants be the first to see new materials; give them publishers' catalogs from which to make recommendations for purchases. Then make a display of the titles when they arrive: "Recommended by the assistants of Everywhere LMC" and place individual assistant's names on the materials they recommended. Let them watch you catalog or repair equipment, explain what you are doing and let them try it. Involve them in the center, share its function, and take them on visits to other facilities. Maybe you could host book talks or learning sessions with guest speakers for "staff only." In other words, treat student assistants as if they were staff members—because they are.

Some schools offer elective course credit for student assistants, but that involves grading the student on accomplishments. With the current emphasis on community involvement and volunteer work, surely student assistants could qualify for such programs. Perhaps businesses would be willing to adopt the program as a cooperative training effort. Perhaps the public library or community college library might be willing to get involved in some way. The local chamber of commerce might work out a job shadowing situation for assistants. The incentives are limited only by your imagination.

The Negatives

If a student does not do the job as expected or takes advantage of a situation, talk to him or her as you would to any employee. Explain the problem, indicate what you want to see happen to correct it, and give the assistant a time period to improve. Then, if necessary, inform the student he or she can no longer be part of the program. If you want to give the student opportunity to try again, consider a suspension with a reevaluation period.

One negative aspect of student assistant programs is that you may not attract the most-qualified workers. Some schools expect special education students to work in the LMC, an excellent experience for them. Unfortunately, there are often detailed tasks that they cannot handle. Other students then avoid working in the LMC for fear they will be labeled "special ed." Such a situation requires recruiting students from the mainstream population to serve as mentors, trainers, or tutors for the students with less ability so that all levels of students can interact.

VOLUNTEERS

The structure, procedures, and plans for student assistants also apply to volunteers. They also need forms, training, evaluation, and recognition. Applications, interviews, and training sessions are necessary for them as well. Because many volunteers are moms, they need to know their efforts can count when and if they seek employment. Unfortunately, some of your best volunteers may become so confident of themselves after working in the LMC that they do, in fact, seek and find outside employment, leaving you to find more volunteers.

A key factor in satisfying volunteers is to make them feel a part of the team effort for educational advancement and improvement. To establish a positive atmosphere

- expect the best
- recognize effort
- give verbal praise
- give feedback
- "brag" about them to others, especially the administration
- maintain a work atmosphere: job descriptions, rules, procedures, and purposes
- adapt situations for individuals with limited abilities or language problems

PAID STAFF

The only difference between assistants, volunteers, and paid clerical staff is money. When someone is being paid to do the work, they are expected to do more. There are also district or building requirements concerning hours, breaks, lunch, days off, etc. There are forms and procedures from the personnel office, probably including an evaluation process, but you may have to add a job description or other forms to make the work experience clearer and more pertinent to the tasks to be performed.

Clerks who have been on the job prior to your arrival sometimes develop the attitude that they know more than you do (and they probably do). Accepting their help graciously while establishing yourself as the one in charge is not always easy. Establishing the same type of process, procedures, and expectations used for assistants and volunteers can be helpful with clerical staff so that both of you know the parameters of your respective assignments. There are job expectations for them—and for you.

Always recognize the value of the staff to you and the program, and let them know you appreciate them. However, do not sell yourself short or allow them to be in charge of the program. If problems develop with clerical staff, remain positive and appreciative, but seek advice from other library media staff or from the administration so the situation does not develop into a bigger problem than it needs to be. Remember, if you let them do everything, they will.

Staff is the key to your success; you cannot do an effective job without some type of assistance. Struggling through your first year alone is difficult, but it does help you understand the full scope of the job. It also may help you figure out what tasks you'd assign to someone else. Begin with the small but time-consuming tasks such as sorting and shelving. Add in processing tasks such as stamping ownership, pasting pockets, and putting plastic covers on book jackets. Using the first year to plan for the assistance you'll seek the next year is a wise move.

16

How do I make people like me?

People relations

In approaching relationships with patrons, the first issue *isn't* getting them to like you. It is far more important that they respect your commitment, admire your persistence, and appreciate your energy. Once these positives are established in their minds, whether or not they like you is immaterial. What is relevant is that they develop a positive attitude about working with you. If your main goal is to make the library media program beneficial to all staff and students by working as long, as hard, and as methodically as is necessary to accomplish that purpose, the patrons will rely on your talents, and anything else will flow from there.

Some patrons are not likable; that doesn't mean they should not receive service and assistance. Their information needs are just as serious and just as important as the information need of the most likable individual in the building. All should be treated in the same fashion. Similarly, you may have some quirks that make you seem somewhat less likable; that doesn't mean you aren't competent, capable, and caring. The issue of liking belongs in personal relationships, and while you deal with people personally as individuals, the relationship should be based on being professional. As a newcomer, therefore, you should think of the job first: of doing the job well, of being a competent professional, and of representing the profession effectively.

SHOWING YOU CARE

There are ways to let patrons know that you care about their information needs and want to assist with those needs. Some of these methods have been covered in previous chapters. It is also worthwhile remembering that interacting with staff really shouldn't be that much different from interacting with patrons. Granted, you may be the supervisor of staff, but a concerned and caring attitude underlies both situations.

The atmosphere of the facility is basic in communicating to patrons that their needs are important. The more patrons feel that the facility is comfortable, convenient, and easy to use, the more they feel someone cares about their needs. All the organizing discussed in previous chapters goes a long way toward letting patrons know their information needs and their ease of use are of primary concern.

A big key to helping patrons recognize your concern is the way they are treated when they enter the facility. Looking up from work, even when it is detailed, lets the individual know you recognize they've entered. A quick smile says welcome. Eye contact encourages discussion, if they want it. It is discomforting to enter a library media center where no one looks at you, no one acknowledges your presence, and your approaching the desk is met with an indifferent stare or, worse yet, a frown. Some specialists do not realize that indifference is just as negative as rejection; neither encourages use. Develop an ability to look open and interested even when you are busy.

Another technique is being alert to patrons' signals. Individuals who are wandering with a puzzled look, who are apparently frustrated, or who are randomly looking here and there may well be individuals who need help and don't know how to ask. Watching facial expressions for such signals, casually approaching people, and quietly asking, "Need some help?" "May I be of assistance?" "Looking for something?" "Everything OK?" tells patrons that you are available, concerned, and aware of their presence. They can then decide if they need your attention or not, but at least you've let it be known you're prepared to give it. This type of watchfulness should apply to all who enter the library media center—whether students, staff, or parents—because it not only encourages dialog but also discourages potential problems.

A third method is to anticipate needs. Some staff members have handled things their own way for so long that they don't ask for or want any help. An alert library media specialist will learn as much as possible about the needs of such patrons, startling them one day with a suggested source or technique they don't know and an offer to help. Studying your patrons—especially teachers—learning their techniques, and being aware of their projects and priorities allows you to develop resources and suggestions to assist.

WORKING WITH TEACHERS

Asking teachers to share their assignments with you gives you an advantage in dealing with both them and their students. You can see not only what is being studied but how it is to be presented. You have a clear picture of the information need, which puts you in the position to suggest activities, identify resources, and develop strategies to assist in fulfilling that need.

Faculty should be treated respectfully as equals. Some may feel superior, some may act superior, some may be superior, but in reality they are doing a job and so are you. Shyly waiting for them to ask for assistance may seem appropriate to a newcomer who doesn't want to appear pushy, but it may also be interpreted as indifference. When staff members are in the LMC, they're on your turf—where you're the one responsible, where your being a good host is natural.

One mistake library media specialists sometimes make is to establish a staff hierarchy in their minds and then act on it. Some abandon teachers when the principal happens by or leave clerks, janitors, and secretaries when a teacher comes in. Such a hierarchy should remain mental and never be demonstrated. All staff members are in the building to do their part: to perpetuate the educational program. An obvious judgment about which role has more value translates to a judgment on people's worth.

When one individual interrupts another's time with you, make a smooth transition from one to the other based on need and nothing else. For example, if a teacher hurriedly enters while a custodian is sharing a comment, break away smoothly and promise to return. "Excuse me, Ms. Montgomery looks a bit frustrated. Let me check with her, and I'll be right back." Thus, neither patron is rejected or judged more important than the other.

Some staff members will demand attention the moment they enter the facility. They will imply by their actions, their conversation, and their attitude that they are a priority. Do not offend them, but do not encourage them. If they interrupt, they need to be told, "I'll be with you in just a second." Resolve the current need to a point where your attention can be shifted. A library media specialist does make and act on judgments, but such decisions should always be prioritized by what is best to advance the library media program.

Some staff members are surprised when they're treated equally and end up as advocates for the program because of it. For instance, when hallway monitors were encouraged to check out paperbacks, the library media staff became heroes. Some staff members expect better treatment because they've always received it, but when they realize the information need determines your priority, they also realize you're doing your job. When a superintendent suddenly appeared in the midst of a busy time when students were looking frantically for information, the library media specialist simply included him: "Dr. Kelly, would you use this source to find information on the Civil War? Jim, tell Dr. Kelly why you think it might help." Suddenly, without expecting it, Dr. Kelly became part of the information need and stayed with the student, learning about the project and the student's search. Dr. Kelly wasn't ignored, but he did not become the priority.

DEALING WITH STUDENTS

When dealing with students, do not abandon their need in order to help a teacher. Do not imply that students have less worth than teachers; after all, if there were no students, you wouldn't have a job. Treat students with the same respect you give to adults. Do not favor one student over another, even if one is more likable or more helpful. Some library media specialists blatantly give priority time and attention to honors students over the needs of students of lesser ability. Not only is this judgment a declaration of one student's value over another, it's ignoring the priority of information need. A student with lesser ability may well need assistance more than an honor student who will probably figure it out without assistance. The spinoff of such action is that the teachers of the slighted students will take note and develop their own opinion of the library media specialist's attitude.

Discipline Considerations

Students and staff need guidance about your behavioral expectations. Publishing such expectations in student and faculty handbooks is one way to let all users know what is expected. Posting behavior expectations is another way to let all users know, deterring some potential offenders and giving others a warning so that you can follow up. For example, if gum, food, and beverages are not allowed in the LMC, post this rule visibly at the entrance. Any offender should politely be asked to get rid of the item. Repeat offenders may be treated with increasing firmness until reaching a point where they lose privileges. But none of them can realistically say "I didn't know."

Students expect structure; many of them respect it and need it even though they may protest. The LMC needs structure so that one individual does not infringe upon the usage needs of another. Students respond to gentle but firm discipline. Again the key is respect. Shouting at a student may get his or her attention, embarrassing the student enough to momentarily curb the behavior. However, the humiliation will not be forgotten by the student or others who observe it. It's hard to convince students they have value when they're treated in a fashion that says they don't.

Respect for individuals and a sense of humor go a long way in working with everyone, but especially students. Instead of telling a perpetual talker who disturbs others that the talking must cease at once, try telling the student "It appears these other students are distracting you. They encourage you to talk, and you can't get your work done. So I've got a nice place over here, away from them, where you can work in peace." The student gets the hint; so do the others. Chances are the talker will move, and the problem is solved. If not, then you can invoke a tougher approach of assigning seats and forbidding usage for a time period.

Another discipline technique is to give students options and conditions. "You've been talking now for ten minutes, and it's bothering others. You can stop, with no more noise, and remain here, or you can move to that table. It's your choice, but if I need to talk to you again, you lose the choice." This gives the student a chance to save face with friends and makes you less of a bad guy.

Discipline Procedures

Establishing a set procedure for discipline problems is also a good idea, but it should be shared with and approved by the administration. Let's say you post ten expectations of behavior in the LMC. You might also post the discipline procedure or print it up and display it at the entrance:

- First offense—student is admonished
- Second offense—student is moved
- Third offense—student loses privileges for a short time
- Fourth offense—student loses privileges for a longer time, referral to the school disciplinarian and/or letter to parents

Many of the situations thus far outlined occur during nonclass usage of the LMC. When a student is with a class, the teacher is responsible for the class's behavior. If students act up, the teacher should be informed. This can become a delicate situation; no teacher wants it inferred that he or she is a poor class manager. It's wise to discuss expectations with the teachers before they come in and work out together how to handle discipline issues.

A structured discipline approach should not be carried to an extreme that constricts the atmosphere. There are LMCs where the primary duty of the specialist seems to be to watch students and catch them doing something wrong. In these centers students who speak, even in hushed whispers, are chastised as if they've committed a major crime. On the other hand, there are LMCs where there are no expectations, and a partylike atmosphere prevails while serious information needs are impossible to pursue. The guiding principle should be the information need as a priority that must be protected. If behavior interferes with that, the behavior must cease. You must be sensitive to this need and ensure its protection.

PARENTS AND OTHER PATRONS

One group many school library media centers overlook is parents. Parents have information needs related to their children. One service you can provide is establishing a parental collection with information on dealing with students of the particular age group. Parents will look to the school for suggestions about homework, drugs, health problems, college, making friends, etc. Providing materials or making bibliographies or working out a joint collection with the local public library lets parents know you are aware of their special needs.

Some schools allow community groups to use their equipment, facilities, and materials. A few have even established hours open to community members so they may use, for example, computers. However, school or district policy may discourage providing equipment and materials to those who aren't students and staff, so it's best to find out what your school's stance is before making the offer.

Unfortunately for some library media specialists, their first significant contact with parents or the community may be because of challenged material. The recent activism of religious-oriented watch groups has especially escalated attacks on school library materials. Handling such a challenge can be a major effort requiring a cool head and support from the library and educational community. The conflict can have dramatic impact on the LMC's public relations, either favorably or unfavorably.

A key thing to bear in mind is that the majority of people raising such challenges, especially parents, are sincerely concerned about a particular piece of material and believe it can damage their child's upbringing according to their standards. Approaching the challenger with the mindset that you are both concerned about the material's effect on children can put you on equal footing instead of being adversaries. Trying to maintain this positive approach is critical, even if it is not always possible.

Figure 16.1 Sample Complaint Form

Consolidated School District #2
Raytown, Missouri
Request for Reconsideration of Books
or Other Instructional Materials

Author: _____

Title: _____

Type of media, if not a book: _____

Publisher or producer (if known): _____

Request initiated by: _____

Street address: _____

City, State, Zip Code: _____ Telephone: _____

Individual represents: Herself/Himself _____
                        Organization (name) _____
                        Other Group (name) _____

- -

If necessary, please use the back of the sheet to complete your answers.

1a. Print. Did you read the entire book, article, publication, etc.?_____
     What parts did you read? _____
     _____
     _____

1b. Audiovisual. If the material in question is media other than a book (film, filmstrip, records, etc.) did you review it in its entirety?_____

2. How was the item acquired? (Assignment, free selection, from a friend, etc.)
_____

3. Is the item part of a set or series? Yes _____ No _____
If yes, did you read, view, or listen to all of the set or series? Yes _____ No _____

4. To what in the material do you object? Please list your specific objections, citing exact passages, page numbers, etc.
_____
_____
_____
_____
_____

5. Did you locate reviews of the items? Yes _____ No _____
If yes, please cite them (source, date, pages, title) _____
_____
_____

6. Did the review(s) substantiate your feelings? _____
_____

7. What effects do you think this material would have on students? Is there any educational or literary merit to the item? _____

_____

_____

_____

8. What do you believe is the purpose of this material?

_____

_____

_____

_____

9. Aside from your specific objections, do you think the book [or other material] has any positive qualities?

_____

_____

10. Would you consider this material to be more appropriate for another grade level? If so which grade level? _____

11. What material would you suggest substituting for the material in question? Please be specific. _____

_____

_____

_____

_____

12. What do you suggest be done with the item in question?

_____

_____

_____

Date	Signature of Individual
Date Received	Received by

Source: Courtesy of Library Media Services Department, Raytown C-2 District, Raytown, Missouri.

Each complaint should be taken seriously, politely, and professionally. Being prepared for such a challenge is the best way to work effectively with it. A sample complaint form is shown in figure 16.1. Promptly give this form to the complainant with an explanation that it is standard policy as the material is reviewed. Temporarily pull the questioned material from the shelves and place it in your office while it is under review. Promptly inform the administration that a question has been raised about an item.

To prepare for such possible challenges, it is wise to have a selection policy in place that has been board-approved (discussed in chapter 8). It is also wise to have a review committee you have set up with the principal's assistance. The committee should include faculty members, the principal, parent representatives, the curriculum coordinator, and yourself. The committee should establish a set procedure for dealing with complaints, including personal review of the item and of the form the challenger fills out.

The procedures the committee will follow and any other pertinent information should be sent to the complainant with an indication of the proper way to proceed. It is important that all participants on both sides of the issue be kept informed about what is happening. (See figure 16.2 for a sample letter to the complainant.) It is equally important, but often difficult, that emotions be kept under control and that the focus remain on the students, the curriculum, and the criteria for the material's inclusion in the collection.

Figure 16.2 Sample Letter for Challenged Materials

Dear

We appreciate your concern over the use of _____
_____ in the C-2 school district. The district has developed procedures for selecting materials but realizes that not everyone will agree with every selection made.

To help you understand the selection process, we are sending you copies of the district's "Collection Development Procedures." These procedures include the:

    1. Material Selection Policy Statement
    2. Procedure for Handling Objections

If you are still concerned after you review this material, please complete the Request for Reconsideration of Material form and return it to me. You may be assured of prompt attention to your request.

If I have not heard from you within ten days, I will assume you no longer wish to file a formal complaint.

Sincerely,

Principal

Source: Courtesy of Library Media Services Department, Raytown C-2 District, Raytown, Missouri.

If a situation becomes especially volatile, which can easily happen, the novice specialist needs to build a support group. Obviously, the members of the committee will be part of this group, as should other area library staff and anyone from the network you've established as discussed in chapter 3. Contacting the Intellectual Freedom Office of the American Library Association at 50 East Huron Street, Chicago, IL 60611, is also a good idea.

The key to people relations is still the golden rule: treat others as you would like to be treated. If you need a reminder of how it feels to be a patron, visit a large library that you don't know. Wander around; try to find materials; request assistance. Take notes in your head and heart about how you feel. Then remember that feeling when someone walks through the door of your LMC.

17

How do I sell the program?
Public relations

For many library media specialists, selling the library media program, marketing it to potential users, and advertising its accomplishments to those inside and outside the school community is one more extra task that seems to be just too much to undertake. Yet as school programs continue to suffer financial distress and public scrutiny, it becomes more critical for all programs within education to meet with public acceptance. The public cannot, will not, accept something it does not understand.

Most people in the general public recall their school library, but it's nothing like today's center. They don't remember the busy place we see today; they don't retain an image of the library media specialist as teammate to teachers, and they don't recognize the vast array of resources the LMC organizes and uses. They don't see these things because that was not their experience. Even those enlightened enough to visit today's LMC, usually parents on open house night, don't fully appreciate what the library media program means to their child and why. Then why should they see this program area as anything other than extra money that need not be spent?

The simple truth today, as it was a decade ago and a decade before that, is that the library media program can survive and grow only in schools where it is recognized as the vital part of the educational program that it is. This recognition must come from staff and students who use it, from administrators who support it, and from a public who understands it. All these target groups must be reminded that the task of educating students is better achieved with a strong library media program. Of course, the best person to remind them, to encourage their support, and to teach them about this great program is the library media specialist—you. That's public relations.

UNDERSTANDING PUBLIC RELATIONS

Public relations is not what many perceive it to be. It is not glossy magazine ads, glitzy TV commercials, or expensive public perception campaigns. It is simple and self-defining: relations with the public. How do the public and the program relate to each other? What does the public—be it teachers, students, other staff members, parents, or the community at large—feel about the program? What does the program do for the public, and how aware are they of it? Are there positive vibes about the program from those who use it and pay for it? An ignorant public or an ignorant section of the public can do tremendous damage out of their own inexperience. It's not personal or malicious or vindictive to be against the expenditures of the library media center; it's just ignorance on the part of a group who know not what they do.

It is up to you to bring all the various sections of the public into an awareness of the program and to develop within them an acceptance and a positive reaction to the program. This is done by informing, educating, and involving all parties—by developing good public relations. Someone once summed up public relations as a two-step process:

- Step 1—do good
- Step 2—tell someone

Library media specialists have, and are, doing fantastic work with step 1. But step 2 is where they falter. Does great work mean anything if no one knows about it?

Students and staff who have a great library media program accept it, then expect it. It becomes as much a part of their routine as reliable bus service. Therefore, they don't brag about it; they don't recognize what is involved to provide it; it's just there. How many of us just accept something that we've come to rely on . . . until it's gone? *Then* we notice how much we need it. Think of TV—how everyone accepts and expects those signals and doesn't even think about them, until the signal is interrupted in the last two minutes of the Super Bowl. Think of how you flip a switch and assume the light will go on, until the circuit blows and you're in darkness. To keep what's vital, we have to remind ourselves of its value *before* we lose it because some things do not come back easily.

When students find the information they need, they should be encouraged to tell someone where they found it and how easy it was. When teachers undertake a unit with the library media specialist as a teammate that results in motivated students and quality projects, they need to be reminded to tell administrators, other teachers, and parents how great it was. Good work needs to be shared, to be passed on to others. Because people tend to remember and talk about their bad experiences in life more readily than the good ones, they need to be encouraged to share the good news.

You must consistently get out the message: We did good work today. We helped the educational program today; we made a difference today. Developing regular activities to get the word out is the best way to start a public relations program. Begin by brainstorming: Write down who needs to hear the message. Next to each group write down one thing you are doing to tell that group about the library media program. Wherever there's a blank, come up with something. Start with one activity per group, then expand it to two activities for each group, then three, and so on.

SOME PR POSSIBILITIES

Students

Ask students to

> create reviews of resources they've found useful or enjoyable; duplicate the reviews, post them in the halls, send them to the school board members, publish them in the school newsletter, send them home to parents
>
> invite their parents to the LMC to be taught (by the student) about a resource in the LMC that the student feels competent using
>
> develop a video about the LMC and its value to them, then show it at an open house and on the local cable channel
>
> create stories or photo essays about "how the LMC saved my day" and make it a regular column in the local paper
>
> prepare trivia questions (and answers) for a local radio show using, of course, the resources of the LMC

Staff

Request that staff

> send letters to parents explaining units to be undertaken in the LMC with the library media specialist as a teammate and inviting them to visit
>
> share a project or idea that worked well with their students as part of a regular column in the LMC monthly newsletter for staff
>
> invite the principal, a board member, or the superintendent to see the results of class work in the LMC or just send the resulting projects to a school board meeting
>
> help create a bulletin board on LMC resources: "My first library visit," "The best source in the LMC," "My favorite book," "Could someone tell me why _____?"

Administrators

Inquire if administrators will

> invite the public to visit the LMC and see what today's education is all about
>
> publish usage statistics in the school or local newspaper
>
> meet monthly with you to find out what's been going on
>
> visit the LMC when an especially innovative or large project is being undertaken
>
> conduct an annual LMC review with you, preceded by your written annual report, to discuss what was accomplished in the current year and what should be attempted for the next year (An outline to help you prepare an annual report is shown in figure 17.1.)

Parents

Encourage parents to

> read regular articles about the LMC's work in general
>
> read the monthly calendar showing which classes are using the LMC for what projects
>
> feel comfortable stopping by the LMC to see what's going on and to use it themselves

The Public

Appeal to the general public to

> visit the library media center in their local school and review a brief summary of its history and purpose
>
> attend special programs each semester highlighting a difference service of the LMC
>
> participate in contests sponsored by the LMC and graded by students to test their knowledge of today's resources and facts

Figure 17.1   Annual Report Outline

Library/Media Department
Annual Report Outline

I.   Cumulated Statistics
    A. Includes any or all of the following:
        1. Circulation
        2. Average number of students per day
        3. Books/software added/discarded
        4. Library skills classes taught or stories read
    B. Overall statistical analysis
        1. Explain the meaning of the numbers
        2. Look for strengths and weaknesses

II. Projects and Positive Occurrences
    A. Major projects completed and their value
    B. Services introduced and an evaluation of success/problems
    C. Special teacher/student instruction
    D. List visitors from other school districts
    E. Professional meetings attended; briefly state how students will benefit

III. Areas of Concern
    A. Be specific
    B. State a plan to deal with problem

IV. Goals for Next Year
    A. Summary of how you met your goals
    B. General statements about long-range goals or projects

Source: Library Media Services Department, Raytown C-2 School District, Raytown, Mo.

A quick look at these lists reveals one common factor: none of the activities can be accomplished without your participation and, probably, initiation. Yet all of these efforts educate individuals about the library media program, involve them in the activities of the LMC, and give them a positive opportunity to meet students and staff and experience what today's educational program can do with an active library media program.

A number of activities are detailed in scores of magazines and books about public relations that you can use to get your message out. The brainstorming list is a quick and easy way to get started. The best plan is to do something every month, preferably for each targeted group.

To focus attention on the LMC, initiate one big project each year that generates lots of involvement with significant numbers of students and teachers and that can culminate in a public program. Whether it's a Renaissance festival, an environmental showcase, an Internet workshop, a student video premiere, or a storytelling festival, find an event that will excite students and staff and will show the public the positive results of a library media program. Above all, don't be afraid to take credit, to get recognition, and to let others know you "done good."

18

How do I keep inspired?

Activities and professional development

As noted in the Getting Started section, a library media specialist has four functions, according to the most recently revised standards:

1. information specialist who acquires and evaluates varied formats of resources and demonstrates locating, accessing, and evaluating information

2. teacher who works with students and others to analyze learning and information needs, finding and using resources for those needs

3. instructional partner who works as a teammate with fellow teachers to help students develop abilities in information use and communication

4. program administrator who manages all aspects of the collection and guides all activities of the program

The library media specialist performs all four functions, even though this book has concentrated on the first and, to a lesser extent, the fourth function. Because it is process and procedure oriented, this manual is geared to the information specialist function. The other functions represent the essence of developing a superior program and should be tackled as soon as the procedural part of the job is under control.

TEACHING

A word might be in order, however, about the teacher and instructional partner roles, which have only been briefly mentioned. Teaching is similar to the old Chinese proverb about a man learning to fish. You can give students the answers to their information needs and their need to know is satisfied for that moment, or you can teach students how to find answers for an information need and their need to know is satisfied for life.

Teaching for the library media specialist encompasses several aspects. There is direct teaching of students individually, in small groups, and in classes. Group teaching includes developing lesson plans, activities, and evaluation procedures as well as following the concepts of good teaching practice. If the school district has adopted a particular teaching model, you should use it as other faculty members do. Such teaching may, or may not, be undertaken as a teammate with the classroom teacher, depending on the lesson parameters mutually developed.

Individual teaching is frequently the most meaningful to the student and the library media specialist because it fosters a closer relationship between the two. Individual contact not only allows concentrated personalized attention but also provides instant response to a student's concern. The interaction that results produces an ever-changing shift in the roles of teacher and learner.

The key to teaching is the need to know. Teaching a student how to use resources, analyze questions, and dig through material to ferret out the right information to answer a specific question is useless unless the student has a need to know. As mentioned previously, that's the reason traditional library orientation and library skills units fail. The students have no need to know, so why listen? When there is a purpose to what is happening, then there is a reason to listen, to try, and to discover. That is the exciting part of being a library media specialist.

INSTRUCTIONAL PARTNERING

Instructional partnering is the way to advance the library media program into and beyond the year 2000. Education is changing, and the library media specialist must change just as teachers must change. Education is becoming too powerful, too over-whelming, too explosive, too big to be accomplished by each person on his or her own. It requires a team effort that always includes the library media specialist, even though the teacher may not understand that yet. The library media specialist demonstrates knowledge of information use and communicates that knowledge to the teacher, working with the teacher to jointly share the process with the student.

You must also know the curriculum and the teaching methods used by the teachers within the building. This knowledge as a background helps you recognize what types of information are needed and how they can be used most effectively. The curriculum is the basis for the selection of materials and the operation of the center. You should participate in curriculum committees, listening and learning about theory and potential changes and developments and acting as a resource for the information needs of committee members as they struggle with decisions that will have an impact on what and how students are taught. As a member of such a committee, you will offer invaluable advice about the availability of resources to activate the curriculum being considered.

Changing the image and the role of the library media program is the responsibility of the library media specialist: *you.* You must move beyond the warehouse function; you must become more than a clerk who simply checks materials in and out and badgers students about overdues. You become a part of the learning process, working cooperatively with teachers. You obtain administrative support for the value of the LMC within the building. You, working with staff and students and parents, define the mission of the library media program. If you don't, you become—or remain—a clerk in charge of a facility that has no direct impact on a student's growth.

It is a huge job—and very difficult to fulfill when you're still trying to find out where the bathroom is, how to operate a new computer, and where to attach the date due slip for a magazine. Every major role created by processes indicated in this text, from choosing an automated system to teaching the research process to establishing procedures to use the Internet, requires more information to make an informed decision. So you turn to professional growth sources. You seek out professional development experiences, relying on fellow professionals to help you find what you need.

PROFESSIONAL DEVELOPMENT OPPORTUNITIES

To get the specific information you need, turn to one, a combination, or all of the following:

> your college connections, whether through continuing education courses or maintaining contact with former classmates and instructors
>
> professional organizations—local, state, and national—for workshops, publications, and conferences
>
> professional reading, both books and periodicals
>
> visits to other, bigger, or better LMCs
>
> networking through LM_NET, other Internet listservs, or people you meet at conferences, workshops, and classes
>
> vendors and publishers that sometimes offer excellent workshops and publications
>
> newspapers and magazines about current events (It's amazing what tidbits in nonprofessional literature can lead to an idea, a statistic, or a philosophy to help you grow.)
>
> role playing (At least once a day don the persona of a student or staff member and look at the LMC, its materials, and yourself from that patron's perspective.)

your own inner self who recognizes the need for the program and is determined to do your best for the students
and staff

Your task will not always be easy. You will become frustrated,
you'll find yourself trying to equalize all roles. (You can't and
shouldn't.) You'll work far longer hours than you thought you
would. (You need to find balance and preserve a personal life.)
You'll become distressed at all you don't know. (But then, who
likes a know-it-all?)

You will also experience a sense of freedom and excitement
you didn't find in other positions. You will find satisfaction in
knowing your efforts made a project work for a class. You'll find
joy in tracking down the answer to that elusive reference question. Finally, you'll realize this position, this job, this profession
has made you marvelously unique.

Epilogue

As mentioned in the preface, this one work couldn't cover all the topics a new library media specialist might encounter. There is a great deal more to learn about curriculum, censorship, joint school-public library ventures, and a myriad of other topics. However, just as you must do with the students, rather than give all the answers, you now know how to find the answers and recognize you will always be seeking information because you are in a job that constantly changes.

Consider the Internet. Today it is vastly changed from what I learned a mere three to four years ago. Then the Web was being discussed and experimented with; today it's mentioned daily in papers and conversations, as much a part of everyday life as the TV. Internet 2 is already beyond the planning stage and will soon be activated, providing a newer, cleaner, faster system.

However, as we expand electronic sources, we must keep our perspective. In a recent contest between resources, a library media specialist found an answer in less than one minute in an encyclopedia while an assistant took four minutes in a specialized reference book and a computer-savvy high school senior gave up after more than five minutes on the Internet. Electronic sources are useful only if their format facilitates easy use. Exploding information can be accessed only if it is set up in a way that makes accessing it understandable. For example, if a database does not accommodate the terms an average individual might use, the source is useless and inaccessible. We need to judge what source is best and to teach how to effectively use all sources.

It is frustrating to watch students print something out from a CD-ROM database or from the Internet assuming their job is done and that somehow the computer "knows" what their need is and can spit it out in one quick keyword search. It also demonstrates the need for the library media specialist, who can teach students how to assimilate, evaluate, and summarize information.

An information search follows a specific process regardless of the source. As library media specialists, we must be constantly aware of the process and work with teachers to show it, use it, and live it with students. We cannot allow the glitz, the glamor, the excitement of the electronic media to overwhelm our common sense. We must recognize that tomorrow's balanced collection refers to types of resources as well as subjects and viewpoints.

Our tomorrow as library media specialists is being written in our actions of today, perhaps more than at any other time in our profession. We can afford neither to live in the past nor to leap off the cliff into the future without checking for a net. We library media specialists are becoming a stronger, wiser, better, more important link between past, present, and future than many of us realize. Are we lucky, or what?

Appendix *A*

Regional Accrediting Agencies

Middle States Association of Colleges and Schools
3624 Market St.
Philadelphia, PA 19104
Phone: (215) 662-5600

New England Association of Schools and Colleges
The Sanborn House
15 High St.
Winchester, MA 01890
(617) 729-6762

North Central Association of Colleges and Schools
159 N. Dearborn St., 6th Fl.
Chicago, IL 60601
(800) 621-7440

Arizona State University
Tempe, AZ 85287
(800) 525-9517

Northwest Association of Schools and Colleges
3700-B University Way NE
Seattle, WA 98105
(206) 543-0195

Southern Association of Colleges and Schools
1866 Southern Ln.
Decatur, GA 30033
(800) 248-7701

Western Association of Schools and Colleges
533 Airport Blvd.
Burlingame, CA 94010
(415) 344-4805

You may also contact
National Study of School Evaluation
1699 E. Woodfield Rd., Ste. 406
Schaumberg, IL 60173
(847) 995-9080

Information Literacy Standards for Student Learning

The Nine Information Literacy Standards for Student Learning

Information Literacy

Standard 1: The student who is information literate accesses information efficiently and effectively.

Standard 2: The student who is information literate evaluates information critically and competently.

Standard 3: The student who is information literate uses information accurately and creatively.

Independent Learning

Standard 4: The student who is an independent learner is information literate and pursues information related to personal interests.

Standard 5: The student who is an independent learner is information literate and appreciates literature and other creative expressions of information.

Standard 6: The student who is an independent learner is information literate and strives for excellence in information seeking and knowledge generation.

Social Responsibility

Standard 7: The student who contributes positively to the learning community and to society is information literate and recognizes the importance of information to a democratic society.

Standard 8: The student who contributes positively to the learning community and to society is information literate and practices ethical behavior in regard to information and information technology.

Standard 9: The student who contributes positively to the learning community and to society is information literate and participates effectively in groups to pursue and generate information.

Source: Draft of "Information Literacy Standards for Student Learning" to be published by the American Library Association in *Information Power: Building Partnerships for Learning.* Copyright © 1998, American Association of School Librarians and Association for Educational Communications and Technology. Reprinted by permission.

Appendix C

American Association of School Librarians Information Sheet

The mission of AASL is to advocate excellence, facilitate change, and develop leaders in the school library media field.

AASL encourages school library media specialists

- to provide leadership in the total educational program
- to participate as active partners in the teaching/learning process
- to connect learners with ideas and information
- to prepare students for lifelong learning, informed decision making, a love of reading, and the use of informational technologies

For additional facts and information, contact:

American Association
   of School Libraries
50 E. Huron St.
Chicago, IL 60611
Phone: (800) 545-2433, Ext. 4386
Fax: (312) 664-7459
E-mail: AASL@ala.org
Home page: http://ala.org/aasl/index.html

AASL activities

National Guidelines: AASL and AECT (American Association for Educational Communications and Technology) have revised and updated *Information Power: Guidelines for School Library Media Programs* (1988). The new *Information Power: Building Partnerships for Learning* is scheduled for publication in 1998. Draft outlines are available on the AASL Web site. Part of this project includes the development of *Information Literacy Standards for Student Learning,* which is available in draft form on the Web site.

Publications: School Library Media Quarterly (electronic), *Knowledge Quest* (magazine), position statements, and a wide variety of books and reports on issues directly affecting the profession.

Special Projects: AASL undertakes special projects funded through efforts with foundations, businesses, and other organizations. Check the AASL Web site for current information. Among those undertaken in recent years:

  National Library Power Program: Technical assistance to the National Library Power Program, funded by the DeWitt Wallace-Reader's Digest Fund. Library Power, an initiative designed to make school libraries the catalyst for improvement of teaching and learning.

  ICONnect: Technology initiative to provide school library media specialists and teachers with training to effectively navigate the Internet and to develop and use meaningful curriculum connections with teachers and students, including mini-grants; KidsConnect, an online question-answer service for students; and an ICONnect Web Site and Gopher.

  Count on Reading: Reading initiative that challenged kids to become avid readers and library users, and school library media specialists to work within their communities to build a nation of readers.

Legislative: Issues affecting school libraries and information technology are addressed through the fulltime ALA Washington, D.C., office staff. For more information visit the ALA Web site or call the Washington office at (800) 941-8478.

While not an official AASL function, stay in touch with other professionals via LM_NET, a listserv/discussion group for school library media professionals. To subscribe, send an e-mail message to <listserv.syr.edu>. Don't put anything in the subject line, and just write "subscribe LM_NET YourFirstName YourLastName" as the message.

Appendix *D*

National Education Goals

By the year 2000

> All children in America will start school ready to learn.
>
> The high school graduation rate will increase to at least 90 percent.
>
> American students will leave grades 4, 8, and 12 having demonstrated competency in challenging subject matter including English, mathematics, science, history, and geography; every school will ensure that all students learn to use their minds well so they can be prepared for responsible citizenry, further learning, and productive employment.
>
> American students will be first in the world in science and mathematics.
>
> Every adult American will be literate and will possess the knowledge and skills necessary to compete in a global economy and exercise the rights and responsibilities of citizenship.
>
> Every school will be free of drugs and violence and will offer a disciplined environment conducive to learning.
>
> Teacher training will be significantly improved.
>
> Local schools will create and develop programs to enlist greater parental involvement in their children's education.

Source: Goals 2000, Educate America Act, 1994.

Appendix E

General Library Media Periodicals

Book Links
434 W. Downer
Aurora, IL 60506
(630) 892-7465

Book Report
Linworth Publishing, Inc.
480 E. Wilson Bridge Rd.,
   Ste. L
Worthington, OH 43085-2372
(800) 786-5017
http://linworth.com

Knowledge Quest
50 E. Huron St.
Chicago, IL 60611
(800) 5454-2433

Library Talk
Linworth Publishing, Inc.
480 E. Wilson Bridge Rd.,
   Ste. L
Worthington, OH 43085-2372
(800) 786-5017
http://linworth.com

School Library Journal
P.O. Box 57559
Boulder, CO 80322-7559
(800) 456-9409

School Library Media Activities Monthly
17 E. Henrietta St.
Baltimore, MD 21230
(410) 685-8621

School Library Media Quarterly (electronic)
50 E. Huron St.
Chicago, IL 60611
(800) 545-2433

American Association of School Librarians' Position Statement on Access to Resources and Services in the School Library Media Program

An Interpretation of the Library Bill of Rights

The school library media program plays a unique role in promoting intellectual freedom. It serves as a point of voluntary access to information and ideas and as a learning laboratory for students as they acquire critical thinking and problem solving skills needed in a pluralistic society. Although the educational level and program of the school necessarily shape the resources and services of a school library media program, the principles of the LIBRARY BILL OF RIGHTS apply equally to all libraries, including school library media programs.

School library media professionals assume a leadership role in promoting the principles of intellectual freedom within the school by providing resources and services that create and sustain an atmosphere of free inquiry. School library media professionals work closely with teachers to integrate instructional activities in classroom units designed to equip students to locate, evaluate, and use a broad range of ideas effectively. Through resources, programming, and educational processes, students and teachers experience the free and robust debate characteristic of a democratic society.

School library media professionals cooperate with other individuals in building collections of resources appropriate to the development and maturity levels of students. These collections provide resources which support curriculum and are consistent with the philosophy, goals, and objectives of the school district. Resources in school library media collections represent diverse points of view and current as well as historical issues.

While English is by history and tradition the customary language of the United States, the languages in use in any given community may vary. Schools serving communities in which other languages are used make efforts to accommodate the needs of students for whom English is a second language. To support these efforts, and to ensure equal access to resources and services, the school library media program provides resources which reflect the linguistic pluralism of the community.

Members of the school community involved in the collection development process employ educational criteria to select resources unfettered by their personal, political, social, or religious views.

Students and educators served by the school library media program have access to resources and services free of constraints resulting from personal, partisan, or doctrinal disapproval. School library media professionals resist efforts by individuals to define what is appropriate for all students or teachers to read, view, or hear.

Major barriers between students and resources include: imposing age or grade level restrictions on the use of resources, limiting the use of interlibrary loan and access to electronic information, charging fees for information in specific formats, requiring permission from parents or teachers, establishing restricted shelves or closed collections, and labeling. Policies, procedures, and rules related to the use of resources and services support free and open access to information.

The school board adopts policies that guarantee access to a broad range of ideas. These include policies on collection development and procedures for the review of resources about which concerns have been raised. Such policies, developed by the persons in the school community, provide for a timely and fair hearing and assure that procedures are applied equitably to all expressions of concern. School library media professionals implement district policies and procedures in the school.

Adopted July, 1986
Amended January, 1990, by the ALA Council
ISBN 8389-7053-2

Appendix G

List of Library Media-Oriented Companies

The companies in this list have proven their interest in school library media programs through their sponsorship and support of the American Association of School Librarians programs, conferences, and initiatives. Many have built a solid reputation for the quality of their products and the dependability of their services. Rather than recommend a specific title—which would be hard to do because there are so many great sources available—I decided to list these companies and let you peruse their catalogs, read reviews, and make your own decision about which ones to select for whatever area requires your further research efforts. I personally recommend you begin with ALA and AASL, but contact others too. Write or call for their most recent catalog and any service/product information.

**American Association of
  School Librarians** (AASL)
50 E. Huron St.
Chicago, IL 60611
(800) 545-2433
www.ala.org/aasl/index.html

  Professional materials

ABC-CLIO
130 Cremona Dr.
Santa Barbara, CA 93117
(800) 368-6868
www.abc-clio.com

  Reference books

**American Library
  Association** (ALA)
50 E. Huron St.
Chicago, IL 60611
(800) 545-2433
www.ala.org

  Professional materials

Baker & Taylor
2709 Water Ridge Pkwy.
Charlotte, NC 28217
(800) 775-1800
www.baker-taylor.com

  Book jobber

Bowker-Sauer Company Ltd.
121 Chanlon Rd.
New Providence, NJ 07974
(800) 521-8110
www.bowker.com

> Professional and reference
> materials

Brodart Co.
500 Arch St.
Williamsport, PA 17705
(800) 233-8567
www.brodart.com

> Automation products and
> services, books and book
> services, furniture and
> supplies

Ebsco Information Services
P.O. Box 1943
Birmingham, AL 35201-1943
(205) 991-6600
www.ebsco.com

> Subscription services,
> CD-ROM products and
> electronic networks

Follett Library Resources
1340 Ridgeview Dr.
McHenry, IL 60050
(800) 435-6170
www.follett.com

> K–12 books, CD-ROMs,
> and audiovisual materials

Follett Software Company
1391 Corporate Dr.
McHenry, IL 60050-7041
(800) 323-3397
www.fsc.follett.com

> Automation systems,
> CD-ROM technology

Forest Press/OCLC
6565 Frantz Rd.
Dublin, OH 43017-3395
(800) 848-5878
www.oclc.org

> Dewey Decimal
> Classification and
> professional titles

Gale Research
835 Penobscot Bldg.
645 Griswold St.
Detroit, MI 48226-4094
(800) 877-GALE
www.gale.com

> Reference materials

**Greenwood Publishing
Group**
88 Post Rd. W
P.O. Box 5007
Westport, CT 06881-5007
(800) 225-5800
www.greenwood.com

> Reference books,
> professional resources

Haworth Press
10 Alice St.
Binghamton, NY 13904-1580
(800) 429-6784
www.haworth.com

>Professional books

Highsmith Inc.
W5527 Hwy. 106
P.O. Box 800
Fort Atkinson, WI 53538-0800
(800) 558-3899
www.highsmith.com

>Library supplies, furniture, and multimedia products

HiWillow Research & Publishing
LMC Source Distrb.
P.O. Box 266
Castle Rock, CO 80104-0266
(800) 367-6770
www.csn.net/~david//

>Professional books

Information Plus
2812 Exchange St.
Wylie, TX 75098
(800) 463-6757

>Current social issues

Libraries Unlimited, Inc.
P.O. Box 6633
Englewood, CO 80155
(800) 237-6124
www.lu.com

>Professional and activity books

Library Learning Resources Inc.
580 Main St.
Chatham, NJ 07928
(201) 635-1833

>Professional books and magazines, reading and science incentives

Linworth Publishing, Inc.
480 E. Wilson Bridge Rd., Ste. L
Worthington, OH 43085
(800) 786-5017
www.linworth.com

>Professional development books and magazines

Microsoft Corp.
5335 Wisconsin Ave. NW, Ste. 600
Washington, DC 20015
(800) 426-9400
www.microsoft.com

>Computer products and software

Neal-Schuman Publishers
100 Varick St.
New York, NY 10013
(212) 925-8650
www.neal-schuman.com

>   Reference and
>   professional books

Oryx Press
4041 North Central Ave.,
    Ste. 700
Phoenix, AZ 85012-3397
(800) 279-6799
www.oryxpress.com

>   Professional materials

Primary Source Media
12 Lunar Dr.
Woodbridge, CT 06525
(800) 444-0799
www.psmedia.com

>   Primary source materials
>   in electronic and
>   microform

SIRS
P.O. Box 2348
Boca Raton, FL 33427-2348
(800) 232-7477
www.sirs.com

>   Electronic and print
>   reference materials,
>   automation system

UMI
300 N. Zeeb Rd.
P.O. Box 1346
Ann Arbor, MI 48106-1346
(800) 521-0600
www.umi.com

>   Electronic references and
>   microform collections

H. W. Wilson Co.
950 University Ave.
Bronx, NY 10452-4224
(800) 367-6770
www.hwwilson.com

>   Reference materials

Winnebago Software Co.
457 E. South St.
Caledonia, MN 55921
(800) 533-5430
www.winnebago.com

>   Automation system

Index

Ann Wasman retired after 31 years in public schools. She was an English teacher, a library media specialist at the junior high and high school levels, and a district coordinator for K–12. She also worked as an inservice coordinator for a special education cooperative.

Wasman copublished *Library Insights, Promotion and Programs (LIPP),* a library PR newsletter, for 15 years and was coauthor of *Grand Schemes and Nitty Gritty Details* published by Libraries Unlimited. She recently edited *Ideas for Promoting Your School Library Media Program* for AASL and worked on the *Know It All* video series for Great Plains National. She has contributed articles, conducted workshops, and given presentations to state and regional associations across the United States. She resides in Illinois with her husband Ben and their two dogs.